To the Creator of Words and Woods
And the inspiration to use them both wisely.

# TREE TO TABLE

## EMERGENCE OF THE URBAN WOOD MOVEMENT

### BY PAUL MORRISON

PAST 9 PUBLISHING

# Tree to Table
## Emergence of the Urban Wood Movement by Paul Morrison

PAST 9
PUBLISHING

Past 9 Publishing
1239 S Fish Hatchery Road
Oregon, Wisconsin 53575
http://www.past9publishing.com

All rights reserved. This book or any portion thereof may not be reproduced or used in any manner whatsoever without the express written permission of the publisher except for the use of brief quotations in a book review.

Unattributed quotations are by Paul Morrison

Copyright 2016 by Paul Morrison

Edition ISBNs
Softcover : 978-0- 9974947-0- 9
eBook: 978-0-9974947-1-6

Book Photography by Elise Marie
Book Graphics by Homestead Designs
Printed Locally

PCN: 2016912397

# TABLE OF CONTENTS

|  | PAGE |
|---|---|
| Chapter 1 \| Defining and Industry | 11 |
| Chapter 2 \| Woodworking History; From Kings to Corporation | 22 |
| Chapter 3 \| Ode to the Beetle | 41 |
| Chapter 4 \| What Distinguishes Urban Wood | 55 |
| Chapter 5 \| Story Time | 72 |
| Chapter 6 \| The Players | 81 |
| Chapter 7 \| Timelines | 98 |
| Chapter 8 \| Know Your Cuts | 109 |
| Chapter 9 \| The Live Edge Phenomenon | 132 |
| Chapter 10 \| A Real World Example | 142 |
| Chapter 11 \| The Economics of Tree to Table Woodworking | 159 |
| Chapter 12 \| Sustainability by Any Other Name | 178 |
| Chapter 13 \| Next Steps | 190 |
| Chapter 14 \| How to Connect | 198 |

# ACKNOWLEDGEMENTS

This ain't the Oscars, but how do you acknowledge all:

- My parents David & Helen and grandparents, Bill & Alice, Gordon & Joyce, for not teaching me to use my gifts wisely, but for instead showing me...
- My wife LaVay, for not thinking me crazy for quitting the comfortable day job with a reliable income for something called a passion...
- The many friends, clients and especially investors, Eric & Sara, the Lutz clan, Al & Carol, and Paul & Roslyn, all of whom fed that passion and in the process also fed my family...
- That same wife who now simply accepted that I am crazy to write this, and yet spent a number of quiet nights listening to a keyboard, followed by a weekend locked in a cabin with me reading pages and pages of a very raw manuscript...
- My peer reviewers, Bruce and Dwayne for keeping the content focused on you the reader...
- My editor Shelby, for taking that somewhat refined content and made it readable to normal people...
- (Story time here: For years I worked with an attorney/ woodworker that would describe the quality of my drafts in terms of sandpaper grit-- -the higher the grit, the better the quality. I am curious to hear what grit we've landed on.)
- My daughters, Brittany and Elise, both accomplished in other creative media, and willing to use those gifts to put life and pictures between the words...
- And of course, the guys back at my shop, Alex, Andy, Jack, Matt, Scott and now Kaleb, for putting up with even rougher sketches and shorter descriptions of the work that still needed to get done while I was off on this writing venture...
- A big thanks to all of you.

# PREFACE

    This book is half story-telling, half documentary and half buyer's-guide. Do the math and you will realize that you are getting a real bargain. You are reading the first book to address an emerging industry—a unique market that requires all three halves; tree stories and old-world craftsmanship all set in a modern day marketplace.

    For those familiar with the farm to table or local food movement, this is it; but in wood. The stories we tell are mostly of trees in the Madison, Wisconsin area near my home. And yet, this book is prompted now by these same stories unfolding across the country. The history I share is likewise Midwestern in origin, but almost of necessity. These small Midwestern farms and neighboring communities are at the roots of many components leading up to this new industry. But again, these roots are by no means a barrier to this industry almost simultaneously emerging from coast to coast and now growing in many of our largest cities.

    Your author, my apologies in advance, is a reformed engineer, turned custom woodworker, urban sawmill operator and small business owner. My wife would argue that all three titles are full-time jobs—and she is not far off. Adding this writing project to the mix is perhaps a bit over the top, but I've been told an engineer that can string a few sentences together without making it sound like a technical manual is not very common. Someone had to write this and who better than someone already doing it—urban wood that is.

    Years back one of my professors wisely pointed out that the formulas and calculations I learned in engineering school would probably not be so important in the long run as the thought process itself and knowing where to find the answers. There are no secret formulas for success and no business calculations on how far this industry might grow. I have intentionally avoided all the technical jargon and market projections. Instead I just present a network of craftsmen with a passion for wood, an eye for art and enough business sense to pull it off. From a global marketing business perspective this may not make sense, but this is exactly how it worked for centuries before us. If farm to table has taught us anything, it has taught us that bigger, better, faster, cheaper need not be the only way.

So where will this book take you?

- I will share a little about how the woodworking industry has evolved over the past century, both from a lumber sourcing and harvesting perspective and from a furniture and finished products production perspective. And then I will present our case for today's urban woodworker.
- I will tell a few stories, some personal and some historical; all with the intent of reminding of us how significant urban trees are in our daily lives, and how important it can be to preserve those memories or that history.
- I will piece together the numerous events and circumstances that came together to launch this new way of doing business. In the process it may look like this was all part of a well-orchestrated market development plan, but those of us in the trenches know better.
- And finally, I will provide the reader with enough information to connect with this movement at any number of possible levels.

This book is aimed at bringing out the feel-good moments of going to a farmers' market or a pick your own farm. The farmer shares his stories about the orchard as you pick your apples, then you re-live those stories with every bite. But here is the trick this book will play on you—the apple trees, or walnut trees or whatever species, they are growing in your yard. The stories are your family stories and the people you meet through this industry we are introducing may be saving your history for future generations.

Just think. When you picked this book up you probably didn't realize you have a lumber crop growing in your back yard. Or be I so bold as to suggest you may have a future dining set growing in your back yard?

# 1
# DEFINING THE INDUSTRY

In my prior life I had a comfortable job in a pleasant office with great staff. I didn't make the best money, but I honestly didn't do so bad either. One of the great aspects of this job was that the hours were fairly well set and it left me with time for my family and both my woodworking and bicycling hobbies.

Then in 1996, I bought a portable sawmill. As I regularly tell people, I purchased the sawmill because I was too cheap to buy good wood. Little did I know how much that sawmill would change my life.

Purchasing a sawmill may sound strange to many, but as you progress through this book you will see that I am far from alone in taking on such an endeavor. With this sawmill, I discovered that I enjoyed sawing logs just as much as building things in my hobby woodworking shop. Essentially the scope of my hobby didn't just grow a little; it started spinning out of control. In just a few months I had sawn many urban logs for friends and neighbors. Within a year the piles were getting out of control.

I had long seen woodworking as a great retirement plan, but with this new option of sawing lumber, I soon recognized the problem I had gotten myself into. It was time to set the keyboard aside, quit the day job, and go turn wood into work.

To turn this idea into a viable business, I theorized that I would just need to seek out the right clients with trees that needed to be removed. We would discuss what we could do with their tree, I would write them a quick proposal, schedule pickup of their trees and return to the shop where I would live out my days in the solitude of humming machinery.

That all sounded like a great plan; a dream that many hobby woodworkers have had. As I started planning my escape route from desk to shop, I learned that leaving my comfortable desk job for what I knew would be a labor intensive and a lower paying trade was not normal. This was one of many 'not normals' I encountered along the path. This network of not normals now has me turning back to the keyboard to share some of them.

This book is about turning abnormalities into a new normal. Why take junk logs loaded with nails and cut them into board using smaller and slower equipment that is located on more expensive real estate than the more remote and more efficient industry counterparts? And then why hire more expensive skilled craftsman from this higher cost neighborhood to build things when there is far cheaper labor available on the opposite side of the planet? The answer lies almost entirely in that last phrase; 'other side of the planet'. That is what this book is about.

But before we get started, I'd like to define a couple important terms.

**Tree to Table Movement** (trē tu̇ tā-blə mu̇v-mənt) *verb*; the overall movement toward urban and locally sourced lumber and finished wood products.

The wood upon which this book is based is lumber sawn primarily from urban trees that had to be removed for any number of reasons. Logs from these urban trees are milled into lumber and dried locally. The lumber is subsequently made into finely crafted furniture and other products; all produced by local woodworkers or craftsmen. These products are most often sold to local customers. This tree to finished product system comprises the tree to table movement. Its parallel is the farm to table movement and a growing network of similar practices focused on the importance of our local economy.

## DEFINING THE INDUSTRY | 13

The whole thing sounds very simple and at a glance you might have assumed this is how things normally happen. Yet, in the global economy, local wood, and especially urban wood is very much a new way of thinking. By the time this book is published, many, if not all, phases of the tree to table concept are likely occurring in your area. However in any particular locale, the various aspects of the movement we will describe in this book may or may not even know their counterparts around them that are fulfilling functions they are seeking. This book aims to change that awareness and improve local networking.

**Urban Wood** (ər-bən wüd) *noun*; wood from trees NOT harvested for their timber value, but removed because of insect, disease or circumstances imposed by the urban environment.

This term is intentionally vague and will likely vary regionally, if not project by project. And that's fine, for a number of reasons, most notable of which is the vast diversity of sources through which this lumber appears.

The reality is that trees grow everywhere and are cut down for an equally large range of reasons. Trying to draw a line between which trees are "in" and which are "out" gets crazy. In most cases, we are talking about a tree that grew in an urban setting, but most professionals in this new industry realize there are also more rurally located trees that come down for various purposes that do not fit the normal scenario of a woodlot owner deciding it's time to harvest lumber.

Let's consider a few examples of urban wood.

The backyard elm once held a long rope swing. In the spring the jute rope shrank several feet from the repeated wet/dry cycles over the winter months, just like a new pair of jeans that lingered too long in the dryer. In April the swing was barely within reach. By August the rope had stretched so close to the ground that your legs barely cleared the ground as you pumped your feet. Then with each summer rain, the swing was instantly a foot taller. One summer when the rope was at a high point, little Paul tried to jump onto the swing, slipped off the plank seat and tumbled to the ground. To add insult to injury, the 2X6 plank came loose and hit the top of my head and I started bleeding like crazy.

This was only one of many trips to the emergency room for my mom, but this tree is where I first learned about harvesting urban wood; but not because of the swing. Several years later, that tree succumbed to Dutch elm disease and needed to come down. Clearly this tree was an urban wood candidate, and it was my first experience with seeing a yard tree turned into lumber.

At that time, however, elm was not as well respected, or dare I say trusted, since it was known for its dramatic movement while air drying. Instead of fine woodwork, this tree became a seawall along Lake Michigan during an era when the lake levels were wreaking havoc on lakefront properties.

One backyard elm down, your author planting tree with elm stump in background and swing tree limb in background overhead.

The park redevelopment plan was intended to resolve a perpetual flooding problem and the aging ash trees were also targets for the invading emerald ash borer. The biggest grove stood where flooding was worst and where the new shelter was planned, so they really need to go. Outwardly they look fine, but arborists also knew the base of several of these trees were decaying from the repeated flooding. The decision was made and they came down.

The wood from those trees still pretty firmly land under the urban wood category. They were from within a municipality and they were removed because of the development plans within that park. Had there been a bigger demand for ash, there may have even been enough to get a logging company in, but for the dozen or so trees there was not enough of a load to justify brining a logging truck into the residential neighborhood.

The powerline dated back to rural electrification era. Most of the old cedar posts had already been replaced one-by-one, but the line itself was old and undersized for all the new development that had been happening in this gradually suburbanizing area. A couple of the trees along this line could probably have been saved, but that would result in a haphazard pole and wire pattern, so the seven old oaks needed to go. A couple of these trees appeared reasonably solid, despite recent tornado damage but others were clearly too far gone.

These were not city trees, so the urban wood title may, at first glance, seem a little more of stretch. There was an old fence line running through them and they still grew next to a cornfield. And yet a handful of iffy storm damaged trees from a fence line are clearly not the stuff of a conventional logging market, nor was their removal for the purposes of harvesting their lumber. The removal was strictly a decision based on negotiations between the utility line, their client neighbors and local officials. We consider this urban wood.

An oak savannah is what the property owner and their environmental consultant saw. Myself, and most others, would have instead labeled this a 10 acre woodlot that 50 years ago was "the back 40." There were a dozen bur oaks and probably twice that many cows at one time. Once the cows stopped grazing, the boxelders, then cherries, hickories and a few other trees moved in. With a shorter growth cycle, many of these trees were now mature while the same old oaks still stood. The site plan called for all but the oaks to be removed, regardless of size.

This is much like the other real world examples above, except it actually describes two recent projects in which we were involved, plus a third site that was now an overgrown city park.

In one of these three cases the sites did not have enough good wood to interest a commercial logger, but the land manager decided it was sufficient for cabinetry and some of the trim and flooring accents in their new home. I would consider this one under the urban heading because the project scale would otherwise have resulted in those logs being discarded.

In the second case, we pre-harvested burled logs and others with "character unbecoming a commercial logging operation", but because the project was both a rural woodlot and of commercial harvesting scale, I don't consider this urban wood. I would instead consider this local wood, if it stayed in the area.

The city park wood became a donation to a Habitat for Humanity project we will describe later, but we considered it urban wood because it was both an urban setting and a planned park redevelopment comparable to the flooding site (just without structures).

And finally, we have the local farmer gone woody. Here in the Midwest, this is actually quite common. Historically, most farms included a woodlot that farmers used for both heating and needed lumber. If there wasn't a mill in the area, one farmer or another either bought or more likely built one and then served his neighboring farms as well.

Over time, many smaller dairy, beef and hog operations

# DEFINING THE INDUSTRY | 17

merged to larger farms, typically still family run, but with greater automation and equipment that made the old wood barns impractical. As metal clad pole barns, electric fences and metal gates became the norm, wood needs also changed. Also, smaller families meant there was less help available to mill the lumber.

The end result is that it became easier to run to the local lumber yard than it was to fell, mill and dry your own wood. Most farm woodlots transitioned into just another crop; albeit a very slow growing crop, periodically harvested by a commercial logger. Most of the small farmer-run mills shut down as the original, second or third generation owners that knew their unique tricks and quirks became too old to run them, or as young mothers refused to let their children help around the whirring 36 inch to 48 inch diameter blades.

Old Circular Mill

Other farmers after, the kids grew and left home, found themselves retiring from their animal operations, but not ready to be put out to pasture themselves. Many instead looked to their long forgotten woodlots and turned to the new era of band saw mills described later. These folks started harvesting wood from their land and quickly found a broader range of farmers and local customers that could use their lumber, or milled products.

This brings us to the third and final definition, at least for now.

**Local Wood** (lō-kəl wüd), *noun*; wood sawn from local mostly non-urban sources.

This book excludes the woodlot owner/manager with a mill from the "urban wood" definition. Instead, we prefer the term local wood. Depending on mill designs and personal preferences, many of these small country mills will accept trees from the urban wood sources described above, and can therefore be considered part time urban wood producers. Others, for good reasons, are more hesitant to do so, since urban wood does come with added consequences that we will cover later. Those mills that decline urban wood likely have experiences that explain and justify their choice of standing clear of urban logs.

But, even if we exclude the small woodlot producer from the urban wood definition, do not entirely discount them. These small mills are a critical part of the local wood market, and should not be disregarded from what I have described as the overall tree to table movement in this book.

Consider the text above and you cannot help but recognize that these small country sawmills with their local clientele represent the remnants of the historical woodworking practices from which the tree to table movement has evolved. To the extent some local country mills will accept urban wood, one must just as quickly accept that an urban sawmill will gladly saw trees from a small woodlot. Honestly, as an operator of a mill that runs more than 90 percent urban logs, we find it quite relaxing to periodically saw a dozen straight, uniform woodlot logs.

The bottom line on our urban wood/local wood distinctions is that we really can't be sticklers on a very unpredictable source stream. Any time we start trying to track the specific details of every log we can probably find a reason to conclude that this log or that one may not be an "urban log." But every time I get into this situation at my shop I end up in the same conversation with myself. If I'm looking at one or a couple logs and can't recall where they came from, the answer is almost certainly that they are urban logs simply based on the fact that there is only one or a couple. On the other hand, if I happen to do a small woodlot harvest (once every couple years), I'll have a pile of a dozen or more logs and I'll have no problem tracking that lot. By their very nature, urban logs usually happen in singles and small quantities.

My recommendation is to use the definitions of this chapter as a framework both for this book and for your conversations within the industry. Yet, I recommend that you recognize that none of these terms are yet firmly established nationwide.

**A Note on Reclaimed, Reused, Recycled, Etc. Etc. Etc. and Barn Wood**

When doing an internet search of the term "urban wood" you will see many listings that really do not relate to the topic of this book. Reclaimed structural lumber is principal among the items sometimes termed urban wood that is not part of our definition. I will attempt to further clarify our scope.

First, this book primarily relates to hardwood lumber. The term hardwood specifically refers to wood produced from deciduous trees; trees with leaves. Hardwood's counterpart, softwood, grows on conifers or evergreens. In general, hardwoods exhibit a greater variation in density, color and grain style as compared with softwoods. There are exceptions, but as a general rule, hardwoods carry a higher value because of these unique species traits. Softwoods are a small component of the urban lumber-making system. In my shop, softwoods represent less than 5 percent of the wood we process.

Second, our primary subject is lumber cut from trees that grew in our lifetime in our neighborhoods, parks and other nearby settings. Structural demolition is a legitimate lumber source, it is just an entirely different lumber source with a different history and different appearances than we will be discussing.

Most structural lumber, both historically and currently, is softwood. One could easily and justifiably argue that the higher density of old growth softwoods is very different than fast-grown pines of today. As I sit typing on a laptop I have my feet resting on a coffee table made from twice reclaimed structural lumber; first a silo, then barn siding. I appreciate the history of this old growth Douglas fir and redwood, but the primary character in this wood is dents, nail holes and weathered texture. This is all character and visible history of what happened during use of the wood, not during growth of the wood. This history can be important and we have connected on some interesting projects involving reclaimed structural lumber. But in this book we are focusing on wood where the history and character within the wood is what happened while that tree was growing.

So as you do that internet search looking for urban wood, you will encounter both projects built from lumber reclaimed from urban structures and projects built from trees that had to come down from an urban landscape for a multitude of reasons and were then sawn into lumber. Many of the craftsmen this book discusses work with both urban wood as defined in this chapter and with reclaimed lumber, so some aspects of this book still apply to reclaimed structural lumber, but this book's primary purpose is urban hardwood trees that need to be removed and subsequently become what we have defined 'urban wood'.

And I mention barnwood just because it is a common sales

line right now. True, historical barn construction reflected the woods of the area where that barn stood; with both hardwoods and softwoods in play. I am a farmboy and have lived and worked with and around farms most of my life, most of which I was also a wood nut and lover of wood framed architecture. I would argue that very few of the products I have seen marketed commercially as "barnwood" have any connection to the types of wood I have seen in barns.

Again, I emphasized that this is still an emerging industry and these terms and examples are not cast in stone. Thinks of them instead as carved in wood; solid wood, but something that can still be sanded and polish around the edges. Behind this movement is a strong network of individuals and businesses that are aimed at developing standards for numerous purposes, not the least of which is defining just what wood we are talking about. With this backdrop of common terminology, we can better communicate why the tree to table industry has formed, what it includes now and where it goes from here.

# 2
# WOODWORKING HISTORY - FROM KINGS TO CORPORATIONS

In the book of Ecclesiastes, King Solomon once said, "There is nothing new under the sun. What is has already been, and what will be has been before." So, anyone who claims to have started the urban wood movement can only speak to their role and their locale, and during their era – your author included. The full truth of the matter is really summed well by this ancient king, author and architect.

I can't speak to King Solomon's exploits with wood, but we do have a fairly complete history of another carpenter from 2,000 years ago who spent his entire career within 50 miles of home. This carpenter was poor, so he likely didn't go the local sawmill to pick out his boards, but instead looked for a nearby tree, felled it, cut or split it, then dried it and made the products his local customer base asked for. Would this work qualify under our urban wood definition? Perhaps, but certainly it was local wood.

What we do know is that throughout history, craftsmen used woods from their locale to make the products they and their neighbors needed. As shipping technology grew, importation of specific species such as mahogany became more abundant, but still local woods were the basis of most construction. Regional forest differences are part of what makes antique furniture so easily distinguished.

In these early American settlements, mills were established on rivers and streams that were dammed for power. Logs were floated to the mills and the start of specialization began. Now some people would concentrate on logging, others on guiding logs down the rivers to the mills and still others ran the mill.

The introduction of the steam engine took this all to the next level. Obviously rail transportation had a major impact on the ability to move wood over more direct routes than the prior river-based system. Small water-driven mills transitioned to larger steam engine mills, still commonly in the same locations, just because the overall infrastructure to support theses mills was already in place. But at the same time, mills could and eventually would move closer to the wood, particularly as local transportation and especially rail transportation expanded to these areas.

We need to add a quick side-note here. While the steam engine started driving toward greater specialization on the overall lumber industry, it also added a more local option. Since mills were no longer tied to the rivers, they could not only move to the big timber areas, they could also move to the farm. As steam tractors started dotting the countryside, so did the farm-based sawmills. These are the mills of legends; large belt-driven blades, some 36" to 48" in diameter started whirring on the most local of levels, with one family or a few neighbors getting together to cut lumber for a barn raising, fencing, or whatever the current needs dictated.

In many regards the steam-driven, farm-based sawmill was the local wood movement of the early 20th century. But those heavy, spinning blades also helped define the risks of urban logs. The big mills were all working in areas of virgin timber that may have gravel ground into the bark, but that could be seen and brushed or chipped off. Embedded steel was something new. These farm-based mills were likely the first to encounter steel, in the form of fence wire or tree fort nails from the yard tree that happened to fall so conveniently just feet from the new mill. So it may not seem very 'urban', but still urban enough to get the point— you don't cut logs that might have steel in them.

These early farm mills were still in the era when most buildings were constructed with the old square or "cut" nails. Cut nails were made from tougher, harder steel than today's common wire nails. If a blade hit this metal it would not only dull the blade, but, because of the momentum with which the blade turned, both the cut nail and broken teeth became shrapnel with considerable speed. Anyone or anything in the line of fire was at considerable risk, and everyone in that line of fire was friend, neighbor or family. The lesson would be learned quickly, either by experience or by word-of-mouth — you don't cut logs that might have steel in them. Even if no one was injured, repairs or resharpening would not be quick.

We will come back to the farm mill again. This is an important part of the local wood/urban wood history, but it is not the main target of this chapter. We were pointing out the early stages of specialization within the lumber industry of the 19th and 20th centuries. And this specialization took off rapidly from the early steam engines to the chain saw era. Increasing degrees of specialization continued to the present time, where now the typical scenario can involve up to a dozen unique hands involved in any wood product transaction:

> **1. Woodlot Owners** | Obviously most wood comes from woodlots ranging from a few acres to vast forests, and nothing the tree to table movement does can, will or even should change this. Many large tracts are owned by timber companies, but even in these cases, the balance of the process still involves all the separate individuals with unique roles, whether under one or many corporate ownerships.
>
> **2. Log Buyers** | In some cases the woodlot owner will specifically contract with a forester to manage the timber sale on their behalf. In other cases, the woodlot owner

will simply contact one or more log buyers and get quotes on the value of a harvest. In a mixed-species lumber harvest, there may be buyers for the overall harvest, then a separate list of buyers for different species or different grades of logs. Certainly for the large corporations that also own land, this role still exists, but instead of being a "buyer" their job duties are to decide what land they will harvest to fill anticipated orders, when each harvest should occur, specifically which species and which grades of logs and what quantity should be targeted in that round, and to which mill the various logs will go.

*Side question: What does a timber buyer see in a forest?*
*Logs on the hoof.*

**3. Loggers** | Third on the scene is the actual guy with the chain saw, a skidder, forwarder and other equipment used to convert trees into a pile of logs at the edge of the woodlot. Again, a variety of interchangeable variations can occur, but rarely is the guy who actually cuts down the tree and moves it out of the woods the same guy who handles the transactions before or after this step.

*Side question: What is the difference between a tree and a log?*
*90 degrees.*

**4. Sawyers (Saw Mill Operators)** | We've now moved from hundreds, if not thousands of landowners, to only a handful of commercial mills in most states that saw and sort the lumber based on the quality and thickness of each board.

26 | TREE TO TABLE

### 1. Woodlot Owners
Individuals or coorporations that own a few acres up to a few thousand acres of timber

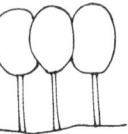

### 2. Log Buyers
Businesses that target woodlot owners to purchase trees or logs of specific sizes and species

### 3. Loggers
Those that cut the standing trees into logs and pile them on the edge of the woodlot

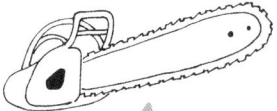

### 4. Sawyers
Those that saw a log into lumber

### 5. Kilns
Those that dry the lumber to make it usable for finished products

### 6. Lumber Wholesaler
A business that sells large quantities of dried lumber to retailers and to large commercial woodworking shops

# WOODWORKING HISTORY - FROM KINGS TO CORPORATIONS | 27

## 12. Client
Those who are the end consumer of the finished product

## 11. Retail Stores
Those that sell the finished product to the end consumer

## 10. Finished Product Wholesalers
Businesses that place high volume orders for finished wood products and fill individual and small orders placed by retailers

## 9. Finisher
Those who take completed wood products and apply appropriate finishes to show the grain and protect the wood surface.

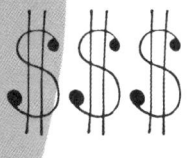

## 8. Woodworker
Those who make lumber into furniture, cabinets and a host of other products

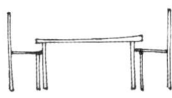

## 7. Lumber Retailer
A local business that keeps lumber on the shelves for hobbyists and smaller local wood shops

Wisconsin ranks among the top hardwood log and lumber production states While a significant portion of logs leave Wisconsin and other hardwood producing states for foreign sawmills and veneer mills, the balance of lumber that is sawn here is milled by about 75 mills that each saw 2 to more than 10 million board feet per year. (A board foot is a volume measurement equivalent to one square foot of wood at one inch thickness.) The Wisconsin hardwood industry considers a mill 'small' if it produces less than a million board feet per year, and any mill that is very much smaller than that becomes irrelevant to the industry. There are literally thousands of portable band saw mills scattered across the countryside, but only a few of those mills produce more than 10,000 board feet per year.

*Side question: What is the difference between a log and lumber? 4 corners.*

**5. Kilns (For Drying Lumber)** | Many of the larger sawmills operate their own kilns and wholesale dried lumber, but this is not always the case. Kilns may be located at the sawmill or may be closer to distribution centers that will later wholesale that lumber to others. Smaller mills are more likely to sell the fresh sawn wet or 'green' lumber to larger kiln operations. Production mills commonly dry 50,000 to 100,000 board feet in each batch, which is more than a typical urban sawmill will produce in a full year.

**6. Lumber Wholesaler** | I call this out separately from the step above, but most often this is a secondary function with separate facilities and staff roles from the kiln operations, but probably under common ownership. This is the warehousing, distribution and marketing end of the lumber production business. Once dried, the lumber is sorted based on a number of quality and size specifications that all relate to market demand. Limited lumber processing is typically part of this step, including rough planing to smooth the surface, making the grain more visible and the warehouse stacks more manageable. Most of these sites also offer additional basic processing and sorting for special client needs. This wholesaler role takes ready-to-use lumber and finds someone who need it. Lots of it. The wholesaler is working with clients that order thousands of dollars in material per month, with a minimum order equal to what a cabinet maker would use for all the cabinets for a home.

**7. Lumber Retailer** | This is the local store shelf we all see. Larger production shops and lumber retailers both purchase in wholesale quantities, then resale single boards and smaller quantities needed by smaller shops and hobbyists.

**8. Woodworker** | Finally, we actually get to making something. This is where the fun really begins for many of us. The project is defined; individual boards are selected and the project takes form. Even here, the tasks are separated in a larger shop, with the design work being done in an office and material preparation in another area by separate staff. The larger shop may further separate tasks, even to the point where the person doing assembly may not have selected which boards are used where, but instead get a pile of parts and an assembly diagram. At this level, wood is just a commodity or another variable expense; a means to the end. Once the fabricator no longer chooses the boards or decides what parts will come from where, artistry is absent from the factory floor. There is no material connection, no local story, just tab "a" slot "b" construction. If tab a and slot b are even parts from the same tree, it is nothing but random chance. Efficiency is paramount, precision is possible (sometimes even better), but craftsmanship has been re-defined.

*Side question: What is the difference between a carpenter and a craftsman?*
*1/16 of an inch (aka: precision).*

**9. Finisher** | While many larger shops have in-shop finishing, many medium and smaller shops outsource finishing. Finishing shops are great and know their stuff, but they are just another cog in what has become a very large corporate machine distancing the grower and the builder from the eventual client.

**10. Finished Product Wholesalers** | Again, on the grand scheme of the global market, distance between the builder and the client becomes irrelevant. The only connection an end user can have with the wood or the maker of their product is whatever connection the furniture store marketing department can create. Specific products are perhaps most often built for a specific retailer, but typically those products still need to travel hundreds if not thousands of miles through a distribution system before arriving at the retailer site or their client's home.

**11. Retail Stores** | Finally, the product is in front of a potential client. In reality, the retailer knows very little about the product or how it was built. Their skill is simply selling a commodity. They know the talking points needed to sell this specific product. They know the margins they have on a regular day and they know how these margins change during their ever-important and frequent "sales". But wait; the piece you see in front you is not likely to be the piece you will actually purchase. More likely, you will get the conveniently boxed copy in the warehouse out back, with complicated instructions telling you how to assemble the piece. The show model and what they have stored out back are so identical that there really is no 'unique character' difference.

**12. Client** | Where would we all be without them; without you? The great thing about these clients is that they keep coming. They may be increasingly frustrated by how often they need to keep coming and they are also increasingly frustrated by sales staff that don't get that 'unique' doesn't simply equate to a better sales pitch. These frustrations are actually just added launching points for the tree to table movement.

A dozen parties in single tree to furniture transaction? Well actually, no; there are probably more like twice that. We skipped right over logistics. A simple word for what used to just be called a trucker, but it is not that simple any longer. Moving from woodlot to dining room requires an entire network of transportation experts with logging trailers, flat beds and enclosed box trucks. And let's not forget boats.

## Imports, Exports and The Wood Industry

When talking about wood furniture production we really need to discuss exporters and importers. The majority of wood products in today's marketplace include an overseas component. Most furniture begins overseas, with only the wholesaling and retailing of the finished products occurring in America. To be fair, I should further clarify— the process does not always begin overseas. Some higher end products start in America with logs or lumber they export from the U.S. before bringing it back here as furniture.

Taking a quick look at the USDA's trade numbers related to logs and lumber for the U.S., we can be proud of this nation's productivity. We send five times as much hardwood lumber out of the country than we take in. That is great and, even with this productivity, many will be surprised to learn that America's forests are growing substantially faster than we are harvesting them. Wisconsin is a heavy producer of hardwood lumber, and yet our forests are growing at twice the rate of harvest.

This growth-to-harvest rate not only considers lumber we use and export, but also logs we export. On the log side our exports are valued at more than 25 times our imports. Again, this is very good from a trade economics standpoint, but the other part of what that means is that while American sawmills are closing their doors, it is not for lack of work. The work is just being shipped overseas.

As you would expect from my comments above, trade in finished products is the exact opposite of lumber. America imports many times more manufactured wood products than it exports. We could spend considerable additional time looking at the details and studying specific numbers related to all this, or we could simply state these differentials are significant, and they represent some very big dollar numbers. If interested in those numbers, a couple starting points are the USDA website or *TradingEconomics.com*.

So, why are we now seeing a change from this highly efficient global system toward local wood or urban wood products that are often processed and crafted within 10 to 50 miles from where those trees grew? There are a number of factors that have all worked together; some in response to problems within the global market concept, others completely independent of those issues.

To start with, specialization comes with many mouths to feed. Ah, the middle men. Every person in the wood product distribution chain needs to bring home a paycheck. Each individual company likely runs their ship as tightly as possible, but then they ship it off to the next guy. Every player looks port and starboard to keep themselves afloat, then transfers their cargo. The net result is a rather awkward system of too many ships moving to and fro, transferring cargo; logs to lumber, lumber to parts and so on. Each transfer costs a few more days, another truck or boat, another forklift operator, just to shuffle on to the next stop. In the end, specialization is proving increasingly inefficient.

One example of the impact of wood moving to the global market is as simple as climate. Those involved in woodworking well recognize the characteristics of wood as a natural product that breaths in its environment. More specifically, it shrinks and swells with the relative humidity of the air around it. Products made in the humid tropics will shrink when they are brought to the Northeast or Midwest. This all makes sense to the woodworker who sets a project aside on a Friday evening, then gets distracted for a week and comes back to dovetailed drawer parts that no longer fit as snug as they did the other day. But this same point is harder to present in a board room where margin is the reigning word of the day, and where moisture is just one of many quality control details that can get lost.

The net result of the globalization of the wood products

industry is that the quality of individual wood products has suffered. It's not necessarily that a craftsman in one part of the world cannot do just as good of work as a craftsman in another part of the world. Instead, it's more a question of the limitations placed on that craftsman and their products, and even the climate they have to work with.

With all the added transportation and fragmentation of the industry, we have each step within the woodworking chain looking for every slight inefficiency under their control to make their slice of the pie just slightly larger. A little trim in efficiency here, a little trim on materials there, just a few seconds less sanding on this part – these are all small corporate decisions to gain a slight edge on the competition. Individually, these revisions are minor, but almost regardless of your personal workshop experience level, you can quickly grasp the cumulative impacts of several parties or even competing departments within an individual company each cutting only minor corners.

Not only does craftsmanship suffer, even the construction materials get trimmed to save money. Look carefully at the specific wording of the sales brochures and you will see a number of descriptions that tread a careful line between accuracy and misleading:

> "Cherry finish" does not mean cherry lumber, it means a color they consider to be equivalent to cherry (but in most cases it is closer to what they believe the customer thinks real cherry would look like).

> "Solids" or "solid wood products" does not necessarily mean wood as it comes from the tree, it more likely means wood chips or sawdust reconstituted into board-like material, then perhaps covered with a real veneer or simply

"oak wood grain finish" also known as plastic.

"Finely crafted American hardwoods" says nothing about where those hardwoods were finely crafted into a product.

We support this economy with every purchase where we look more at the financial bottom line than at the full impact of the product simply because the price better fits our specific need or desire at that moment. Once this slippery slope began, the majority of wood furniture production industry fell into the hole. Those that have not are increasingly challenged by the ever-increasing price disparity between their standard production system and the cheaper quality and prices of their mostly overseas competitors. Even several well-known and respected brands that have tried to hold to their quality standards have still shipped productions overseas to improve their competitive stance in the global market.

**…Versus, Tree to Table**

So why should we not all join the world of specialization and globalization? Where is the problem? If the customer is still coming to the door, why not simply accept that this is how things are and will be? It is, after all, we the consumers are accepting the increasingly more disposable furniture and other products that were traditionally called 'durable goods.' The answer; we have found a better way. The tree to table movement is that alternative. It simplicity can also be diagramed in a manner that does not take two pages, a dozen players and a fleet of trucks and ships.

Now, as it turns out, this is not such a new model after all. It is really just a restoration of the old world economy where tree source, mill, builder and buyer were all neighbors. In that economy it is not simply everyone looking out for how to cut the corners as far as possible, it is an economy where every player knows they will be seeing all the other players again regularly, both as repeat supplier or customer and as the source of their next referral. We will return to this concept repeatedly, but for now simply admire the simplicity of this marketing model.

**Tree to Table Model**

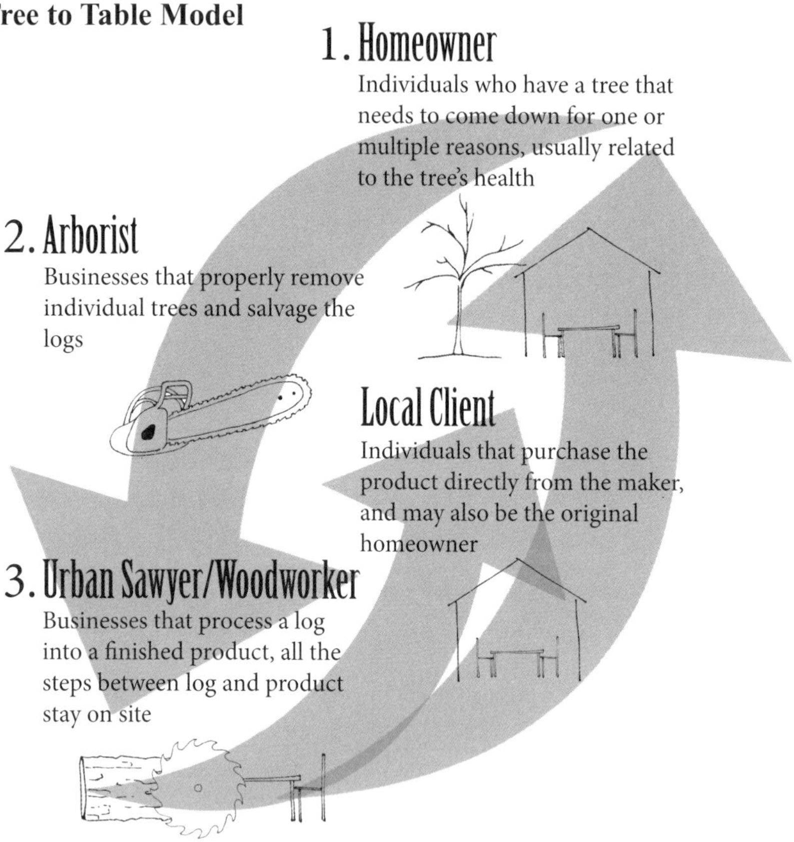

### 1. Homeowner
Individuals who have a tree that needs to come down for one or multiple reasons, usually related to the tree's health

### 2. Arborist
Businesses that properly remove individual trees and salvage the logs

### Local Client
Individuals that purchase the product directly from the maker, and may also be the original homeowner

### 3. Urban Sawyer/Woodworker
Businesses that process a log into a finished product, all the steps between log and product stay on site

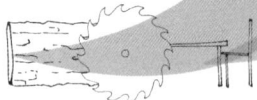

**The Amish as a Global Economic Player**

     I am guessing that sub-title caught you off guard. Maybe even suggesting this is dangerous ground, but while I am on my soap box, I might as well raise the question.

To be fair, we are still talking American made for the American marketplace, but in all other regards the patterns of the global economy are much the same. With agricultural commodities all fully incorporated into world economics, small Amish farms have not fared well and agriculture has become a decreasing revenue stream within the Amish economy.

Woodworking and other building trades and services that were once grandfather/father/son businesses scaled to serve their own communities and their immediate neighbors have become production-scale shops that increasingly dominate the Amish labor force. Some such businesses are Amish owned and managed. Others, such as the recreational vehicle industry of northern Indiana and Ohio are simply located in surrounding communities and have come to depend on the strong family bonds and work ethics of the Amish laborer. The RV industry is the perfect example of the Amish labor force aimed at a marketplace far beyond the Amish network.

To make this system work while maintaining their cultural traditions, however, has required greater connections into the same global market we already discussed. Obviously each sect follows a unique set of rules, but in general these shops run the same types of equipment as other small to medium sized woodworking shops, but commonly without connections to the electrical power grid. They instead power their equipment using gas or diesel engines running either electrical generators, compressed air systems or hydraulic systems. None of these systems can come close to the energy efficiency of nation's electrical power grid, but make no mistake that they are all products of our global economy.

But how can an Amish worker thrive in a world economy dependent upon its phones, computers, cars and trucks? All these capabilities are beyond the picket fences of our idealized pictures of the Amish craftsman working in his unplugged shop. Quite simply, the Amish have plugged into the non-Amish economic system by partnering into a network of non-Amish marketing experts that have successfully developed "Amish" into just one more brand name. We now have extensive multi-state distribution networks and transportation systems to shuttle lumber, raw products and finished works from mills to workshops to 'independent' stores located in nearly every larger metropolitan area that tout the Amish brand name.

The Amish market system is entirely consistent with the broader world market model, right down to the brand identity of a consistent logo. The network has developed a complete product line with pre-defined styles and pricing parameters. And, in the Amish worker, they have found the best and cheapest workers available. The beauty in all this is that workforce itself and the images of old world craftsmanship it conjures up in our American mindset IS the brand.

Personally, I appreciate their efforts to separate from distracting if not destructive aspects of modern society. I much admire their aversion to borrowing and more of us should adopt these principals, since that alone would substantially improve the bottom line for both businesses and families. As a farmboy myself, I also cannot think of a better way to learn a solid work ethic than growing up in an agricultural community with strong family values.

At the same time, I must admit I don't quite grasp the concepts of fully employing some modern technologies while dis-avowing others. There seems to be a similarly broad range of viewpoints within the Amish culture. I've met an Amish woodworker as he was driving his diesel bobcat skid loader up the driveway after picking up his mail, and yet his fields were plowed by horses. We then stepped into his off-the-grid wood shop with piles of sawdust and perhaps half the factory-supplied guards. He then flipped out his Bic lighter to ignite an open flame propane lantern connected to the same propane bottle you would use for your gas grill. Nowhere else in America could I encounter such dichotomies. The growing uncertainty of how to apply social programs like unemployment, workers compensation and even OSHA standards to a culture within our country that disavows those concepts as counter to a family's responsibility are likewise creating increasing confusion within the Amish community.

We can also appreciate the conceptual connection to the history of the local farm-based sawmills but even that connection is more conceptual that actual. Some wood certainly originates from their local farms, but as the brand has grown, less and less of the lumber is grown or produced local. Much, if not most, is from the conventional kiln-dried commercial lumber market.

Unfortunately, even the range in product quality I have observed in outlet stores pushing the Amish brand has stepped farther and farther from the traditional view of the expert craftsman than the marketing materials declare. Yes, there are exceptional Amish craftsmen, just as there are exceptional urban wood craftsmen and exceptional craftsmen dealing with exotic hardwoods from all over the world. But most Amish production shops are not much past their first generation and, as these businesses simply become an employment option instead of a passion, quality can suffer. Or as these craftsmen are told they need to meet a certain price point, quality can suffer. Or when today's project is just another piece headed to the loading dock instead of to a face-to-face client, quality can suffer. Does this not all sound familiar?

## And It Is Not Just the Wood Product Buyer

Those of us who are woodworkers are also part of this economy. Fewer and fewer tools are built here in the U.S. and we are item by item purchasing tools from the global market, sometimes because of cost, sometimes because the American counterparts no longer exist.

Within the woodworking community there remains a fascination if not preference for "old steel," specifically referring to equipment made in America over the past century that is still working or can be readily repaired or rebuilt by local machine shops. I likewise bow to this fascination if not preference and am currently excited by an old Yates planer I have acquired but not yet placed into service. I must admit a bias here—the Yates name is part of my family tree (by marriage some century ago). Is my own shop all American made equipment? No, but about 75 percent is because I am more likely to buy good used equipment over new equipment.

Globalization of the woodworking industry over the past century is not at the center of this book. Trade deficits and even 'Buy American' are not my point either. There are plenty of other books, studies and slogans around those points.

My point in this chapter is to simply identify an unfortunate trend within the greater economic system that has also infected the world of woodworking that many of us care so much about. The history of woodworking is filled with far more positives than negatives and many of those positives still remain in various corporate models.

Yet, this recent woodworking trend is very relevant to the issues of this book. So let us simply stop here and accept that a less than ideal scenario has developed in recent years. Instead of ranting we will look at the plethora of opportunities our circumstances have planted to aid the growth of an emerging tree to table movement. This is the result we are focusing on and the brief history I am sharing is merely canvas behind our growing tree to table masterpiece.

# 3
# ODE TO THE BEETLE; FROM "GOT WOOD" TO .ORG

As the quality of many wood products decreased, the stage was being set for the emergence of the tree to table movement through a number of other circumstances. No one detail and no individual or group can be credited with the concept. Instead, a combination of ecological, technological and societal factors all came together to launch this ship.

**The New Home**

As we went through the 70s and 80s, the baby boomer generation was moving from starter homes and starter incomes to bigger homes and larger disposable incomes. During these transitions the cheap assembly line furniture helped to fill the affordability gap. As those products rapidly reached the ends of their brief life cycles these boomers realized that much of the furniture they purchased was not standing up as well as the antiques passed down from prior generations. By the turn of the century, sound craftsmanship was becoming sorely missed and the demand for quality started returning.

Today, I have seen this unfold among my clients, my peers and in my own home, piece by piece or room by room as the updates occur. Some homeowners move in the direction of antiques and want their own custom pieces or their kitchen cabinetry to blend in with these classic works. Without question, much of the current demand for finer craftsmanship comes from those who have studied the designs, joinery and overall workmanship of past generations. This sense is so strong that many of the craftsmen I know consider themselves antique makers – our pieces are just very young antiques.

In other homes, this transition takes a more contemporary path. Interestingly, this more contemporary look with its own version of clean lines sometimes looks to wood, and especially the natural flowing forms of live edge wood to bring warmth back into what can otherwise become a sterile or cold look.

Regardless, fine woodwork is in demand, and often the demand cannot be met by antiques or "factory custom" design options. I find it both satisfying and frustrating that the term "custom" is so revered that it is now impossible to purchase kitchen cabinetry that is not considered "custom." It is great to see that consumers desire works that are truly customized to their aesthetics. The consumer still recognizes and values craftsmanship. This desire has helped propel the few remaining one-man and very small custom shops into today's tree to table movement.

Unfortunately the term "custom" also fell prey to piracy by the global marketplace. "Custom" is now used to describe factory produced boxes that are machine cut to standardized dimensions, with pre-defined options on species, profiles and finishes. The individual boxes and designs are rarely unique, but are instead simply catalog options sized on 3-inch increments of width, depth and height. In most cases, the sequence in which these boxes are organized as they are placed in a kitchen is the only "custom" component of the mix. The loss of this once valued term is perhaps the greatest reason the true custom woodworker sometimes feels the need to define their work. Urban wood is becoming one such distinguishing elixir.

**The Chainsaw Mill**

Backing up to the 1970s, an early foray into urban lumber

production began with the marketing of chain saw attachments that allowed slab or board cutting with a chain saw. These mills, commonly known today as Alaskan mills (one of the brand names), consist of a set of bars or panel that was affixed to a larger chain saw. This allowed the operator to make parallel cuts with the chainsaw. The chain saw mill introduced three new concepts:

- Sawing lumber with the portability of a chain saw. Previously if you wanted something sawn, bringing it to the sawmill was the only option. The portable chain saw mill concept provided the option of bringing the mill to the saw.
- Consumer level sawmilling. While not fast, the chain sawmill concept at least provided an affordable alternative to convincing a sawmill to saw an individual log, and especially an individual log that might include steel. Now what is worthy of sawing and how could be decisions made by the log owner and all on their timeline.
- A reduced cost and peril from hitting steel. We've discussed how hitting steel on a large circular mill is both expensive and dangerous. While chain saw use is still accompanied by risk, both the degree of risk and cost of replacing or sharpening a chain that hit a nail became much lower when compared to a production sawmill.

Chain saw mills have become the tool of many woodworkers that have stumbled upon a tree too good to turn into firewood. They have been used on countless back yard trees and in remote woodlots for pieces just too heavy for a woodworker to carry out any other way. They are still an important tool of the urban woodworker. I have one and use it regularly. But a chain saw mill is just too slow and too wasteful for conventional lumber production, so it is more the tool of the hobbyist and the business that cuts very large slabs that we discuss later. Still, all these concepts played into the next generation of mills.

## The Portable Bandsaw Mill

The farm scale circular mills provided a great counterpart to the big mills by making small woodlot and local sawing common. With time, a few mobile versions of these mills also emerged. However, neither these farm-based circular mills nor their more mobile counterparts were compatible with logs that contained steel commonly found in urban wood.

The portable band saw mill would change this and become a critical component to the tree to table movement. Woodmizer first introduced their mill in 1982. That introduction opened avenues for people to bring production sawmill capabilities to the log and to then cut in a manner that was safe and efficient, with blades that were affordable and replaceable.

Nails and other hardware often found in urban wood can still stop the cut of a band saw mill, but the hazard of literal shrapnel associated with a 4-foot diameter whirring sawmill blade were gone. The cost of hitting a nail went from well over $100 in time and materials lost to a repair (and risk of limb and life) to a five-minute blade change and a $25 blade. If the blade was not damaged too bad you could also re-sharpen.

Woodmizer and their many soon to follow competitors, made custom sawing and even on-site sawing commonplace within a decade. As an added side-benefit, a band saw blade is less than half the thickness of the traditional circular mills, so less wood is wasted on each cut.

But even the improvement in band mill designs alone were not enough to jump start the tree to table movement. Thousands of these mills were sold and have produced massive quantities of lumber. In most cases, these purchases began with a need for

Woodmizer, 1982 to present (by permission)

lumber and an opportunity to get logs that could become lumber but, often these mill operators eventually found themselves sitting on a pile of lumber they did not need and did not know how to sell. My current Woodmizer mill was one such story. I (indirectly) bought the mill from an arborist who saw value in the logs they cut down, but subsequently found difficulty finding a market for that lumber. Thankfully, combined with other factors below, those markets for urban wood are now growing.

**Farm to Table**

We owe more to this local food movement than just a word. Food quality issues and nation-wide recalls due to contamination caused at various levels within a huge food processing industry helped fuel a very fair question – what ever happened to just getting your food from the farmer down the road? That is not to say that the same contamination concerns could not happen more locally, but the fears and efforts are different when your food transactions are producer to user instead of the following process:

- The farmer loading food on a truck destined for some remote

processing center.
- The trucker transporting that load, then cleaning his truck for the next pick-up.
- The food processing center worker waiting impatiently for their shift to end.
- The next warehouse and trucker both trying to maintain a certain temperature setting and delivery schedule whether the roadway is sweltering or snow-covered.
- The grocery store unloading that truck and trying to keep track of a million products on their shelf, each with an expiration date.
- Or the restaurant worker that lost track of which container just arrived and which one has been sitting there since last week.

The producers and consumers who have partnered to form the farm to table movement have established a sincere respect for each other. They are just growers providing their best efforts. They are not part of an overly complicated system delivering food to consumers. Moreover, many consumers recognize there is more to food management than a stamped expiration date. And they all seem to make it work without a parade of attorneys. Doesn't that sound kind of old-school?

## The Great Recession, the Buy Local Economy and Social Media

There are many aspects to this section, but at the center is that same "whatever happened to" question answered by the farm to table movement. A number of big picture details and individual personal crisis circumstances all occurred in such a short window that their combined impact is shifting how we shop. We all entered a worldwide economic recession and emerged with an understanding that sometimes the local option may not be the cheapest option, but may still be the best option.

    Consider all the people who were suddenly without a job and with no prospect of finding one soon. Many realized they could make a few Christmas gifts by putting their woodworking hobby or other hobbies into production mode. Then they recognized through new social media tools that they could take this trade beyond the confines of immediate family. When their lumber inventory ran low, they may have just gone to the local lumber yard, or they may have found out about this guy with a mill. And, as it turns out, that guy with the mill is also struggling in the economic downturn and is now making a new effort at selling that pile of lumber he has been sitting on since buying a bandsaw mill. Both of these people and many more were gaining a greater interest in supporting other local businesses. Entire organizations are now formed around this buy local idea.

    Meanwhile, as social media evolved and became more prominent, applications were developed specifically to share creative ideas. Suddenly an idea from one person in one locale shows up on the other side of the country. People see the idea on social media and think 'I like the idea, but the guy that made it is either unidentified or five states away. Who do I know in my area that can make that unique product?' That person then checks their local network, builds a new friendship and that leads to the next project, and on it goes.

    Of course, this extremely simplifies the entire concept and the social dynamics behind the buy local movement, but I am an engineer/woodworker, not a sociologist. The end result is all I am looking to grasp. The 'great' recession is in many ways just that; great. Not only has it hopefully taught us some fiscal restraint, but it has given us a new appreciation that not every product has to come from some unknown source elsewhere on the planet. The best source for our next need might be just down the road.

## Emerald Ash Borer or EAB

And finally, we come to that stinking emerald ash borer – the beetle that came over on a boat also helped launch the buy-local movement. We can and should be upset by this devastating ash killer, but, at the same time, the response to discovery of the emerald ash borer in the Detroit area in 2002 played a significant role in the tree to table movement of today.

Ash has always been a relatively abundant wood in the upper Midwest and eastern states. Its native range sweeps across most of the country from Montana to the northeast and south to near the Gulf Coast. To those familiar with it, ash has long been one of the under-represented hardwoods, perhaps because of its two-tone lumber, perhaps because it is too similar in appearance to red oak. In many ways, however, emerald ash borer has become an urban issue and especially a municipal issue. To put this into perspective, we need to go back to the major urban wood related crisis of the prior generation – Dutch elm disease.

Elm was the perfect yard tree and the perfect city street or park tree for much of America, transforming streets into cathedralled passages. They were tough and flexible with a long life, and their natural shape meant few low hanging limbs. Their leaves were abundant for shade, but relatively small, so they didn't clog storm drains.

When Dutch elm disease started taking its toll in the 1950s and 1960s, replacements were sought both for established neighborhoods that lost their elms and for a thriving building industry that was planting entirely new neighborhoods for the baby boomer generation. In the Midwest, ash and honey locust were deemed the best options. These trees offered many of the same characteristics of elms and had no known threats. In many neighborhoods and parks, ash became "the" street terrace tree.

It would be nice to think the massive die-off of elm trees would have taught us the virtues of species diversification, but unfortunately this was not so. It became too easy to go with the best known species and soon ash was an over-represented percentage within our urban landscape. Then EAB was discovered and within a couple short years we learned that EAB was not just here, it was already well established, having landed in many port cities and simultaneously spread to the surrounding neighborhoods. The first trees likely died and became firewood distributed throughout the surrounding areas before a connection was made to the new green bug on the scene.

EAB is not the only tree-destroying discovery from foreign shores. Gypsy moth was also well on its way across the nation by this time, impacting oaks and other hardwoods, but at a slower rate of destruction. The Asian longhorn beetle was also found in several ports. This much larger bug with a less selective appetite was more than willing to attack our maple, birch, poplar, beech, ash and willows, but has fortunately been confined to smaller areas and, at least in theory, eradicated in some.

I find it both ironic and disappointing that some of those crates carrying the "disposable" furniture we discussed in the prior chapter might also have been the source to the pest problems American hardwoods now face. Is it not appropriate that the tree to table movement, which runs counter-culture to the world economy, might stem, at least in part, from a problem created by that world economy?

Yet we cannot only look at foreign pests either. Perhaps the pest of greatest concern to many within the wood industry is native-born. Thousand canker disease was once a limited-impact concern for walnut in a few western states, but has recently been found in eastern states, home to the bulk of our world supply of black walnut, North America's highest value hardwood. This new concern also falls back to transportation of infected wood from its native setting across natural barriers that limited it impact. Thousand cankers could well be the biggest wood issue our country ever faces, and its prevention also favors a more local woodworking economy.

**Responses to Emerald Ash Borer**

As we were learning the extent of EAB's spread, municipalities quickly realized that the ash trees they were still planting in massive numbers were now at risk. This begged a couple important questions – How many ash trees had we planted in our urban settings and were we facing the same urban tree crisis of the prior generation? We quickly learned that the answer was yes.

Without question, ash is a substantially over-represented species in many urban settings of the eastern U.S. Detroit and a number of other cities where EAB was first found had little time to react and within a few years, they were into a wave of heavy tree removals. As news and photos shared the impact of EAB in those first cities, other municipalities reflected on the devastating impact of Dutch elm disease and recognized their need to make a plan.

Many individual state natural resource agencies entered into this effort; both recognizing the impacts on their forestry industries and on municipalities. Obviously widespread testing for infestations was a first step for state agencies, but tree inventories were a good starting point at the municipal level, sometimes co-funded by the state agencies. A quick search on the internet reveals many of these study results and I was quickly able to pull up the following statistics.

# ODE TO THE BEETLE; FROM "GOT WOOD" TO .ORG | 51

- Des Moines, IA: 6,000 street side or right-of-way ash, 47,000 on municipal land
- Chicago IL: 85,000 (17% of all right-of-way trees)
- St Louis, MO: 11,200 (14% of right-of-way trees)
- Albany, NY: 1,000 street side or right-of-way ash, 1,200 on municipal land
- Florence, KY: 13% ash of all street tree species
- Gastonia, NC: 19% ash of all street tree species
- Toledo, OH: 9% ash of all street tree species
- Harrisburg, PA: of the 6,828 trees inventoried 64 were ash species
- Nashville, TN: of the 2,060 trees inventoried 31 were ash species

  Without much more effort, you can likely find the results for nearly any community. I asked the public works director in our small town outside Madison and he was able to rattle off a specific count without even pausing to think about it. Why are these numbers so immediately available? The answer is quite simply that many municipalities realize they have a significant task on their hands; if not now, at least sometime in their near future.

  Baltimore, Maryland takes this to another level. With a naturally high ash forest concentration, the city has an estimated 293,000 ash trees, within its boundaries and approximately 6 million in the metropolitan area.

  In Madison, Wisconsin, where I am based (21,700 right of way ash), the city and several other organizations have worked with the Wisconsin Department of Natural Resources to survey the status of municipal ash, and to explore options for utilization of the wood once EAB progressed to the area.

  In one older, well established Madison neighborhood, a community group used a state grant to conduct a survey identifying every tree within that neighborhood, both public and private. That study found 24 percent of municipal trees were ash and 13 percent of private trees were ash. In reviewing the report we notice that many private trees are smaller ornamentals, so the true canopy impact on private land is greater still.

Both public and private property percentages are many times the ash percentage of rural Wisconsin. This is also a neighborhood that was built well before Dutch elm disease rolled through. Some ash was of course already present, but many more were added following Dutch elm losses. Madison, as with most growing cities, has many newer neighborhoods that were just corn fields at the time Dutch elm rolled through and the ash percentages in some of these 30 to 40 year old neighborhoods are likely even higher.

**Moving Beyond Assessment**

In Ann Arbor, Michigan, Recycle Ann Arbor and the Southeast Michigan Resource Conservation and Development Council decided to move EAB plans to the next level. As an established recycling center for other materials, they started an effort to reclaim not only ash, but other urban trees. They partnered with local sawmills to have these logs sawn into lumber. Beginning in 2006, Recycle Ann Arbor with four partner mills started offering wood from the urban landscape for public sale at their site. The response to this new product offering was exceptional.

Habitat for Humanity is well known for their home construction projects, and has developed a network of re-sale stores called ReStores focused on used and left-over building supplies. Revenues from the stores are used to help support Habitat for Humanity's house building projects. They also had an existing client base of people with a sustainable bent, and that were already looking for wood. By 2012, Recycle Ann Arbor connected with

Genesee County Habitat for Humanity ReStore and duplicated their original model by offering urban wood from the Flint, Michigan landscape at that ReStore. The Michigan network has continued to grow from there, with at least 10 member mills and product producers as of early 2016.

In 2008, Cincinnati began an urban wood utilization program. The Cincinnati Park Board, Cincinnati Public Schools and Hamilton County Solid Waste District pooled efforts to take urban ash from city property and then utilized a local private sawmill and a local wood products manufacturer to produce school furnishings. Those furnishings now double as an instructional aid – showcasing what grows in the local community and is produced by local manufacturers.

**Events to Emergence**

The projects above are by no means the only coordinated efforts that have resulted from emerald ash borer. Instead they are representative of a growing pattern. In large part, the tree to table movement is simply a conglomeration of many circumstances and coordinated efforts all aligning – new product innovations, consumer frustrations with declining product values, both world and local economics, and a new wave of craftsmanship. All of these details were progressing independently and many still are. The mere existence of EAB, however, has increased public awareness of our urban timber and simultaneously provided a host of opportunities for these individuals to start collaborating. In many ways, we are also realizing the "competitor" down the road can also be a partner if we look at our individual business strengths and weaknesses.

If you can follow my logic here, think of it this way: emerald ash borer, the stow-away in the pallets of the global market's cargo ship, caused the perfect storm, which in turn helped launched the tree to table ship that, in the end, is beginning to turn back that global market. Or in Dr. Seuss terms; "all because a little bug went ka-choo."

Ode to a beetle? Perhaps we should title this chapter "Owed to a beetle." How interesting that in this era of sustainability, even our most dreaded pest should be green.

# 4
# WHAT DISTINGUISHES URBAN WOOD FROM THE REST?

The reality is that wood is more distinguished by species than by source. City oak and country oak are much the same, and neither the tree nor its lumber looks like walnut or cherry.

Likewise, a good log grown on a woodlot would still be a good log grown in a back yard. And yet there are many ways in which urban wood differs from its woodlot counterparts. These distinctions are where we will focus.

When I get calls from homeowners about a tree in their yard I begin by asking a series of questions. "Can you get your arms around it?" "Can you reach the first limb?" (To be completely honest, if I am in my office I am also probably looking up the address on Google Maps to see if I can get a street view of the tree while we talk.) My intent in both is to get a sense of whether their particular log sounds like it might yield good lumber. If the questions or street view indicate otherwise, I am less interested. My reality as a businessman is that not every tree is worth the effort it takes to reclaim its wood.

But, as a guy who has spent more than 20 years sawing hundreds of woodlot logs and thousands of urban logs, I have to say there is a second half to the story. Urban trees, the uses they serve and the eventual logs and lumber they produce, tend to have certain characteristics that make both the wood and the processing of that wood unique.

**Hardware**

This could be its own chapter, and for those wanting to dig

deeper into this, there is much to be learned. Those of us sawing urban logs have seen and heard so many stories about things found in trees that we are not surprised by the next guy's story, and yet we still love to hear them. We will share a few as we go, as examples of the more common things that the urban sawyer must watch for, but please feel free to submit your own experiences to our website *www.past9publishing.com.*

Metal fence post in burl box elder

People love their trees in different ways. Unfortunately, one of the most common ways is to pound something into them. I know this sounds criminal to the sawmill operator, but it goes with the turf. A sawmill operator (sawyer) like myself looks at a tree and sees a "log on the hoof" – a living version of what they will someday saw. So we cringe at the sight of hammock hooks and spikes holding tree fort ladder steps. We simply need to look away and repeat the words "highest and best use." Homeowners, municipalities and arborists are right to recognize the highest and best use for an urban log is attached to its stump with leafy branches above.

Unfortunately, for both the arborist and sawyer, many of the uses these trees serve include nails, wires, screws and bolts. Trees are natural posts, and far more solid than any post one can plant in the ground, so the bottom six to eight feet of many urban trees contain steel from signs, fences, clotheslines, dog runs, hammocks and just about anything that requires a sturdy post.

The good news about steel is that most uses, other than a tree fort ladder, only take a few fasteners and most are within reach of the ground. The bad news is that bottom eight feet of the tree typically offers some of the best lumber. The other bad news is that the tree has likely survived multiple generations and may have nails at various depths over time.

There is some predictability with steel, in that it is most common in the residential backyard, less common and generally only smaller nails in the front yard tree, and least common in the city park tree. If you saw urban logs, you must be willing to accept the impacts of steel. We can go days without hitting a nail, then hit five in a single pass. It is simply part of the turf.

Another curious part of tree-care history was a historically common tree repair method of filling voids with concrete. One red elm we worked with had a 75-pound block of concrete filling a void between two limbs that was fully healed over. Yes, thanks for asking, that was a chain saw blade destroyed. However, the three dining tables we pulled from that tree still made the overall project worthwhile.

Interestingly, that same tree with 75 pounds of concrete at 12 feet off the ground also had an old-fashioned auger bit embedded in the tree several feet above the concrete. All that remained visible was the telltale square tip that would be inserted into the chuck of the crank-style brace. I know this tool could have been used by an arborist doing tree reinforcement, but I doubt an arborist would have left a bit half-embedded in the tree. Personally, I suspect a young child was playing with dad's tools while building a treehouse and got it stuck but didn't want to tell dad. I may be way off, but it sounds like something I might have done as a kid.

The biggest concrete fill we've seen so far was inside the largest and oldest oak on the University of Wisconsin-Madison campus. Known as the President's Oak, it was well over five feet in diameter at chest height, about the same height where there was once a hole large enough to stick a hand inside. When it came time for removal, that hole was grown over. The tree service started with their big saw and soon hit 'something' They switched to a second saw and attacked from a different angle, again hitting 'something.' By the third saw they were able to remove a small wedge and see a free-standing concrete pillar inside a four-foot diameter cavity at the center of the tree. After its removal we discovered a pillar of concrete more than four feet tall and 16 inches across.

Concrete pillar inside President's Oak

There are, of course, other metals embedded in trees that are not quite as hazardous as steel. I think it's safe to say most sawmills – urban and rural – have encounter bullets in trees. I know I have – I once kept a jar of them. However, after we got a target practice tree from a farm the novelty quickly wore off.

In one of those oak savannah restoration sites I mentioned in Chapter 1, I encountered a cherry tree covered in pitch (hardened sap). The woodlot had a number of trees with unusual

and highly desirable figured growths call burls so I imagined the tree may have some
interesting grain. However, once that log hit the sawmill I learned the rest of the story. As it turned out the sappy tree was really the perfect target practice tree for a nearby deer stand. A dozen bullets appeared in each of five slabs we cut from the tree. That's not a dozen bullets total, but a dozen in each board. I'm still debating the best use for these slabs.

    I discuss the risks of hitting objects with a sawmill, but the obvious question is what about those that the sawmill misses and makes it into the woodworking shop? Is that not also a risk? Yes, we cannot ignore this possibility, and we need to be alert in the shop. I'd particularly caution the wood turner who is picking his wood based on unusual shapes on the tree – these shapes might be growths that are concealing hardware. Yet in all our years of sawing and hitting nails and bolts at our sawmill almost daily, I can only think of one occasion where we missed steel right up to it hitting the knives of our planer. That is not bad for more than 1,500 completed projects and well over 100,000 board feet of urban lumber milled.

    In the end, the best that can be said about hardware and urban trees is that you don't know what you might find. I know of a tree that is coming down soon with a short length of thick plastic rope sticking out the side about 15 feet up the tree. I have no idea what it was for or what it is attached to, and neither does the owner or the neighbor whose home it faces. We will be cutting above and below the rope on that tree.

    In another instance, we were surprised by what we didn't find. We received an oak tree from a client's backyard and, as we were sawing, we ran into a void in the tree. That is not uncommon, except this void was perfectly rectangular with two nails at the bottom of the hole. Apparently the tree once had a 2x4 nailed to its side. The tree grew around the 2x4, almost completely encasing it before it rotted away. All that remained was a perfect 2x4 void and the nails that held it.

Expect the unexpected and you will find it in an urban tree.

## Character

     Now there is a term to define. One of the first things we hear from buyers of our urban wood is that they love the unique character of the wood. It almost sounds illogical, but with the extreme efficiencies that the commercial wood market has built, it is increasingly difficult for the custom woodworker to find high character wood in the conventional lumberyard.
     There are a few specific character traits that are defined and marketed, such as "curly" and "birdseye" and a handful of other terms, but any truly unique or one-of-a-kind character is unlikely to ever find a retail shelf. I cannot help but speculate that part of the interest in buying expensive foreign exotic woods is simply a desire to find wood that is different.
     The lack of character wood in the marketplace is because much of the character contained within trees are considered defects

in the traditional lumber grading standards. None of us typically want defects like splits or twisted boards, but bizarre grain and unusual mineralized colors, unique knots, bark inclusions, pitch pockets and a variety of other unusual character traits can be the details that make a product unique.

For instance, I have a set of tables in my showroom with tops cut from a common American hardwood. This particular log contains a grain pattern that I cannot describe other than to call it different. I've had several experienced woodworkers ask me what kind of wood it is only to be surprised to learn that it is cherry. Someone will see the unique character of these tables and decide they are exactly what they are looking for; even though neither they nor I have ever seen cherry that looked like this. In fact, that unique character will likely be the specific reason they buy them.

That said, what makes the overall character of urban lumber unique? Is it simply that urban sawyers don't sort the lumber by commercial grading standards, or is there more to it? The answer is both. In my work, I view myself as a woodworker first, a sawmill operator second and a lumber dealer third. The primary purpose for my mill is to serve my woodworking business and my woodworking business needs character wood. I can go to the lumber yard if I just want straight, uniform grain, but so can any of my competitors. My market edge over these other shops is wood with character.

Obviously my mill, or any other urban mill, loves uniform, straight logs and will mill these logs to yield the highest grade lumber possible. But, even in these urban logs, some differences can occur in how they are managed:

- If the board comes off my mill unusually wide, it stays unusually wide until it is used. I see no sense in trimming a board narrower just to remove a 'defect' that someone might

later decide is a 'feature'. As a woodworker myself, I'd like to make that decision, so the board stays wide until it hits the shop floor. This seems very logical, but it is contrary to the large commercial mill's best interests.
- Likewise, when I encounter a board with a knot dead center on length and width, I don't cut it into two short boards with no knots. Might not my custom shop want a board with a unique center knot? That board stays whole.
- If we are half way through a run of logs that we were planning to make into inch boards and we find something unique inside the next log, we will set it aside and talk with the owner of that log to discuss a new set of options. Live edge, unusual coloring, pitch pockets and stains from wood acids interacting with metal are all reasons to pause for a moment and consider whether an otherwise ordinary log might produce something better.

The urban tree sawyer is much more likely than a commercial sawyer to welcome and accept logs with unique characteristics. In other words, when the good logs are done, so is the big mill. Low grade logs are usually never sent to the big mills. They are instead separated at the loading area on the edge of the woodlot, then sent to a pallet maker or a mill that just runs flooring.

The urban sawyer intentionally seeks out large and unusual logs simply for the character we know they contain. When I have the opportunity to see a tree before or while the arborist is working, I'll advise them on the cuts I would like to see made based on the shapes I see and the projects I can imagine.

Once these less-common logs reach my mill, both my shop and most other urban sawyers I know, assess the log to determine what will make the most unique option from that wood. To this extent, urban lumber simply has higher character because urban sawyers seek out what the wood provides based on a different market approach.

**A Tree Without its Forest**

The overall architecture of a tree or the shape of its primary structural members also impact wood character. Within their natural environmental settings, each tree species has its typical structure. Urban trees tend toward a unique architecture that lends itself to a different look; both for the tree and its lumber.

On the savannah, the bur oak has a short, stout trunk with branches spreading as wide as the tree is tall. Its close relative, the white oak, is more typically found in a woodlot, with incredible height and rarely a single surviving limb within 30 to 40 feet of the ground. A white oak is not typically found on the prairie, but when it is, it will be shaped by its surroundings to look more like its bur oak cousin than its brother in the woodlot.

Bur Oak (prairie grown)     White Oak (woodlot grown)

Likewise, growth rates relate directly to the tree's environment. All plants look for sunlight, moisture and nutrients and in any given setting for any given season, one of these three will be the limiting factor. Genetics combine with these limiting ingredients to determine the rate of grow, and rate of growth in turn determines both strength factors and grain character. For my purposes as a fine woodworker, strength is usually less of a factor and grain character is an important factor.

    The woodlot tree gains its tall, straight height by competing for light. There are often plenty of nutrients in the soil from decaying leaves and limbs of past trees and the cool shaded soils are usually moist here in the Great Lakes region, but light is only abundant some 80 to 120 feet above those rich soils. Anything that helps that tree draw closer to the light strengthens the tree; anything that detracts from this goal is a waste of energy and decreases the chance of survival. Low hanging limbs are a distraction from the main goal, so they tend to wither and die. A double trunk requires too much energy for one root system, so that tree will also will fail to thrive or die on the woodlot.

    These same woodlot trees may not be native to a prairie setting, but in the open prairie a tall, thin trunk is a liability both for wind and lightening. If the woodlot species is grown where light is always and everywhere present, height is not important. Instead, the low side limbs that become useless in the woodlot, can instead thrive in the side-light, feed the tree and grow immense. The only limitation is whether the structural ties between those limbs and the trunk can support the weight of those wider and heavier side limbs.

    Similarly, urban trees are also affected by their surrounding environmental factors. Generally speaking, most trees that are planted in an urban environment experience something more like the prairie setting than the tightly-packed competition of the woodlot setting. Even a two story house casts a small shadow compared to what that tree would see in a woodlot, so in most cases urban trees have the wider profiles of prairie trees.

    The difference between the urban and prairie settings is that the tree's characteristics are determined more by owner preference than by nature. For instance, trunks are at heights determined by the property owner's convenience, not by grazing deer, elk, antelope, buffalo, or the occasional wild fire or holstein cow.

At the same time, what buildings do provide is shelter. In the prairie setting strong winds can prune young trees through brute force. Only structurally appropriate and well profiled limbs survive the strong winds of an open prairie. Sheltered by buildings, young urban trees can over-populate with limbs and those poorly structured forms can become substantial before reaching heights significant enough to be impacted by a severe urban wind.

The result is an urban tree with multiple stems and with limb densities and junctions that are not normal in nature. This is where the profession of an arborist comes to the forefront in defining a revised set of growth parameters for trees in this new environment. With proper pruning, care and eventual reinforcement, these trees can be guided or outright reconfigured by an arborist to serve their primary urban purposes well. Yet, when these trees do come down, the unique shapes can offer character that is hard to find in their native woodlot counterparts. This is the stuff of urban logging.

Pruning itself can lend a unique trait. Trimmed limb cuts that have healed over can lend some interesting grain patterns. I once had a slice taken from a tree that grew outside the state Capitol here in Madison. That particular slab was a perfect cross-section of a limb cut, fully healed over. I simple framed the board and took it to a show with a title plaque of "VETOED". It sold before I got a picture.

**Size**

There are big trees everywhere, but many of the biggest hardwoods you will ever see are not hidden in some remote woodlot. They are in a back yard, on a golf course, or even in a cemetery.

In Wisconsin, and in many other states, there are champion tree lists that identify the largest trees of every species that are known with that state. There is even a national champion registry that can be viewed at *www.americanforest.org*. These champions are both a fun claim to fame, and also registries that guide others toward opportunities to see some truly remarkable trees. I live near several and check them out whenever I get the chance.

A quick look through the Wisconsin listing shows three of every four champions to be urban trees. Obviously many of these trees are ornamentals, so the total counts are bias toward an urban setting. Yet, even among the more recognized lumber species, well over half the known champions are urban.

While specific locations of the national champion trees are not defined on the website I mentioned above, a quick glance at those trees with photos reveals easily one third of them appear to be urban settings. I also venture that few, if any, of these champions will eventually fall to the chain saw for the purpose of a timber harvest. Instead, they will more likely meet their demise in other fashions, more in line with our definition of urban wood.

The fact that champion trees are more common in an urban environment should come as no surprise. A champion tree is one that is prized by its owners, whether urban or woodlot. If it's in a yard, owners typically do whatever is needed or affordable up until the point that it must be removed. A listed champion tree in a family farm woodlot is also more likely to be bypassed by it owner's request during a commercial harvest. In a larger, commercially managed forest, that large tree might simply be viewed as a commodity ripe for harvest and likely has long since gone to the mill.

Among the largest of the native Wisconsin trees are bur oaks. The big ones often go back more than 200 years; well before

Wisconsin was a state. Bur oaks are the classic prairie oak trees. Many still grace farm fields and fence lines and some still reside in their native or restored prairie settings. However, by address and locational descriptions in Wisconsin's champion tree list, all the listed champions would be considered urban. They are either located directly in an urban environment or in a farm yard, where they will continue until they need to come down for reasons other than a simple harvest.

When it comes to urban wood, size matters. Champion status considers three criteria, height of the tree, breadth of the limb spread, and circumference of the trunk at four and a half feet off the ground. This third measure is also the measurement a forester uses to determine a tree's potential lumber yield. The diameter at four and a half feet off the ground is called the diameter at breast height or DBH and is a convenient measure of a log that discounts the over-sized root flare and better represents what the log will yield in lumber. On a shorter urban log this measurement may be less accurate or representative, but it at least provides a comparable standard measurement.

For instance, for live edge designs, size defines possible uses. When a single slab from a tree can make a full table, size also impresses even after the tree is down. Even a pair of slabs from the same tree makes an impressive table – likewise, with bar tops, countertops, kitchen islands, all the way down to coffee and end tables. When you combined the grain character of wide branch unions and other features more common in the urban tree, the artistic possibilities are seemingly endless.

Nowhere does size matter as much as black walnut. Walnut is already among the most valuable trees to those of us who too frequently look at a tree and see "lumber on the hoof," so they deserve a special note.

Single-slab bur oak table     "Bookmatched" Walnut Table

    Most large walnut trees, especially the veneer quality walnuts from a woodlot, bring such incredible prices that they are out of reach for the average woodworker or local sawmill. Much of this highly prized wood simply disappears overseas. In an over-specialized global market, each individual within that market looks to how they can best profit. The logger sees a special log and calls the veneer buyer. The veneer buyer looks to who is willing to pay the most, which is usually a buyer somewhere overseas. Some local live-edge aficionado might be interested in a couple logs and might pay well, but 'just a couple' is not part of the global economy's volume-based system and not worth the extra hassle for a commercial log buyer.

    In my experience, the biggest walnut trees are in the urban environment. This is not because they grow that much bigger in a city, but because in a woodlot they are more often viewed as a high-value commodity, so they get cut more quickly. For the urban walnut, the same rules apply as mentioned for the champion trees – they stay because they are enjoyed. I can easily point out a dozen walnut trees in urban areas within 20 miles of my shop, each one of which far exceeds any woodlot walnut I know.

## Unique Species/Exotics

How many kinds of wood can you name? Not the imported exotics, but just the woods that are part of our everyday woodworking vocabulary that you could find at some local hardwood dealer? If you can name more than a dozen you are doing well, and have a well-stocked lumber dealer.

Now, how many kinds of trees grow in your neighborhood? Not just the big oaks, ash and maple, but all the trees, including the ornamentals that may not be any bigger than a couple inches in diameter that may still be of interest to supply some local woodworker. Next, include many of the variants on these species where what is under the bark may have distinct properties, or may simply be interesting because it is that specific variant. You've probably just exploded the number of lumber types you can imagine by several fold, if not by an order of magnitude. Add to this the character variants from the prior section and –boom, we have an almost infinite range of possibilities.

Exotic wood need not be something imported. It might be as close as your back yard. The floor of my showroom has nine different woods, only half would be considered common lumber species. I've built kitchens in hackberry, butternut and black locust. I've heard stories about how pin oak is a low quality lumber, yet I just had breakfast with friends at our dining room table made from a book-matched pair of pin oak slabs.

Bur oak is supposedly a non-preferred version of white oak, and yet we built two dining room tables that were four feet wide and ten feet long, each from a single slab for clients that preferred the character of bur oak over walnut. I've done coffee tables from boxelder and both headboards and tables in honey locust. Norway maple is often considered an undesirable invasive, but I can tell you it makes a stunning desktop.

For several years we have been supplying urban lumber to areas woodworkers through a couple local Habitat for Humanity ReStore locations. One point we have learned from this market; any wood that grows in Madison sells in Madison. I don't know all the projects this wood is being used for, but if it grows here, somewhere in town a woodworker wants to use it.

Many of these same trees are also found in woodlots, but with such a low frequency that they are often ignored. Hackberry, for example, is one of those neglected woods that even the commercial lumber market is starting to recognize. It is native throughout the eastern U.S., but nowhere is it abundant.

When I first got a hackberry, I did it by mistaken identity. It grew just a few miles away and a friend mentioned a huge ash was coming down, so I stopped by to ask the tree service if I could have the log. I was still checking out the size of the log and observing where they were making their final cuts when a guy from the tree crew asked what I did with hackberry. Honestly I had to tell them I didn't know yet, his question was the first time I noticed the bark was not that of an ash tree. I just saw another hackberry that uprooted in a strong storm over the past week and am probably more excited by this log than by the three oaks I'll be picking up tomorrow, or (dare I say it) by the walnut I picked up last week.

A commercial logger is prone to ignore the less common oddities, simply because they are harder to find a use for in a marketplace focused on high-volume species. Yet, oddity is exactly what many custom woodworkers specifically seek. Unless a log buyer can find a large number or has a special buyer in mind, the random stray species in a woodlot will be viewed as pallet lumber because their value does not justify finding an interested sawmill.

The combined result of greater species diversity in the urban setting and less competition from the traditional lumber market bode well for the urban sawyer. We can offer a huge range of exotic woods with names that are not only familiar to the woodworker, but also familiar to their clients – names familiar because they know they have such a tree in their yard. At the same time, these people are awakened to the idea that their own tree might be a candidate for such use when it needs to come down.

# 5
# STORY TIME

One thing I've learned as I've worked with urban wood is that wood tells stories. As I attend art shows and furniture shows, either as a vendor or in discussions with other fine woodworkers at such shows, a host of "common tree/uncommon wood" topics always come up. While I represent one of a growing number of businesses that specifically focus on urban wood, many fine woodworkers have found themselves roped into or drawn into a backyard log extraction event and then gone through the full cycle of processing the wood into a finished product.

Why? Sometimes it is the allure of a unique piece of wood. Sometimes it is just to see the results. Sometimes the process itself creates a sentimental attachment to the finished piece. Other times the sentimental attachment is already there in the form of a tree with special meaning or memories. I regularly talk with home owners that watched their tree grow, and eventually watched with regret as the tree faltered. Many times I'm hearing these stories from the person that planted the tree, or their adult child.

I can't begin to share all the tree-related stories I have connected with over the years and mine are just one set of stories from one wood business in one community. Following are an assortment of those I've found most enjoyable.

**Squirrel Cage:** I once had a very unusually shaped walnut log that clearly had survived some damage and re-healed, leaving a large scar. Once I cut the log I discovered the tree had a substantial void behind that healed scar. The void had been scrubbed clean by squirrels and contained a sizable stash of walnuts all encased by newer growth over the void.

**The Monkey Tree:** In the early 1960s the monkeys escaped from the Madison zoo. Some rumors are that the attendant failed to latch the gait, others venture it was a fraternity prank, and the third version is that both are true (there may have been multiple escapes that year). Regardless of how it happened, the result was a number of monkeys scattered throughout the adjoining neighborhood. Some were on the lamb for several months.

One such tree was enjoyed by a family of five young boys. The large bur oak, had a cast iron clothesline pulley attached to its side that doubled as a porch-to-tree transport for those boys (when mother wasn't watching of course). That tree, as evidenced by its many nails, was also host to multiple tree forts. The morning of the monkey escape the boys awoke to find monkeys in their tree. What could be better for a family of young boys than monkeys in your tree fort tree?

The initial monkey escape was of course a subject of much media attention in its day. After we completed a dining set from that tree (it recently died), another local columnist was given an opportunity to retell the original story roughly 50 years later. The steel pulley (now fully encased by years of new wood grow over it), has been located, and will soon be a table for one of those young boys, (now nearing retirement).

**Tornado Tree:** Every year the Midwest faces a number of tornadoes, most of them from late May through June. On August 18, 2005, Wisconsin had a record 27 tornadoes in a single day. The worst of these was an F3 storm that left a path of damage 20 miles long and centered on the outskirts of Stoughton, Wisconsin. The storm damaged and destroyed hundreds of homes, completely leveling more than 20.

Before converting my current facilities, my shop was a barn that was twice struck by tornadoes and a third passed by within a mile as we were building our house. The Stoughton tornado first touched ground just a couple miles past our shop and home. The power at our home was knocked out just as they were announcing the storm and we would later realize the storm cell responsible was passing overhead at that very moment. This was before smart phones and our radio batteries had gone dead. Once the storm passed the skies immediately cleared. With no power inside we just sat outside watching a spectacular cloud formation to our east. We had no idea what devastation was occurring below that cloud.

We later learned a former co-worker had lost their home in that storm. As we were enjoying our peaceful evening, the roof and walls of their home were being torn away and the floor was literally flapping in the wind as they huddled in the basement. When it was time to do cabinetry and woodwork for their new home, we used the remaining parts of a backyard walnut as accents for the cabinetry, staircase, mantle and bedroom sets. The primary wood for those cabinets was quarter-sawn white oak from another tornado to hit Madison the year before their home was destroyed. For the record, that house has now stood more than a decade without further tornado issues, as has my shop.

**Corporate Symbol:** The Madison area is headquarters to a nationwide company whose product line is successful because of the stories they tell. Several of those stories, although fictional, point back to an old bur oak tree, a real tree that once stood at the corporate headquarters. That tree was part of their corporate identity and its gradual demise was viewed so tragically they would simply rather not have their loss publicized by being named here.

Corporate symbols, of course, are not allowed to die. So when the oak eventually succumbed to old age, environmental stress, gypsy moth, or really a combination of all these, we were asked to preserve the tree by making their board room table, storybook shelves for their remote production facilities, turned bowls for the founder and current president and several smaller employee gift items.

**Anniversary Tree:** A bit younger on the oak list, one nearby couple celebrated their anniversary by planting an oak tree given to them by their parents. This tree only lived about 45 years before its death, but the children of that couple wanted to preserve the memory of both their grandparents and parents by having us mill the tree and build a dining room table for their new home.

**"It's why we bought the house:"** This is actually a conglomeration of stories that we have connected with, including the monkey tree story above. We've all heard realtors say location, location, location, but they could just have easily said trees, big trees, wonderful trees. Healthy mature trees add substantially to a property's worth. Likewise, dead or dying trees can substantially reduce a property's value, both because of the removal cost and because of the visual hole that the tree leaves behind.

## Capturing History

If you had not noticed before, the last couple pages should make it clear that this book is as much story telling as it is a dissertation defining the tree to table movement. That is intentional. It will come up again and again as we proceed. I mentioned in a previous chapter that the size of a tree is important to my trade, but stories are even more important. Success of many businesses is simply their ability to tell a story. Need I name names, or do they simply come to mind?

Trees play such a cherished role in our lives, both as children and as adults, so it should come as no surprise how valuable it can be to preserve these memories. Building products from the very trees they are connected with is an unbelievably effective method of doing so. I know. I'm sitting and typing at a table that brings back memories. I look up and see another table that brings back different memories. I glance to the side and see a lamp my grandfather made and it brings back more memories. What are family heirlooms? They are memories. Why not turn the family tree into that heirloom piece?

As I exhibit at shows and start sharing the stories connected with the products I am exhibiting, I almost always have at least one couple say "I wish I would have known about you when…" Oh, the opportunity lost. But just as often I hear "I have this tree…" Oh, the opportunity gained. The most recent show I attended I heard the former line twice, but the later line five times. Yes, my main goal at these art and trade shows is to sell things that I have made and recover costs already invested. Yet every time I hear "I have this tree…" I'm further reminded of the opportunities still ahead for the tree to table movement. With that, I must take this story issue one step farther. Sometimes it is not the story specifically, but the history more generally that is important. To explain, a couple more stories.

**Wisconsin State Capitol Lawn Bur Oak:** During the Civil War, Madison was home to the Eagle Brigade, a Wisconsin regiment with a bald eagled named Old Abe as its mascot. After the war, when the famed eagle died, it was preserved and placed in the state capitol. That capitol later burned to the ground, with the preserved mascot inside. The capitol was rebuilt more elegantly than its original, and now boasts the second largest domed capitol in the nation, just four feet shorter than the national capitol. When another bald eagle was found dead, it was preserved and used as a replica for the original. This replacement is now itself over 100 years old and sits in a Civil War museum inside the capitol, roosting on a bur oak limb.

Madison is perhaps a bit too well known for its protests, and the "best" place for a protest in the city has always been on the capitol steps facing State Street. These steps facing the University of Wisconsin-Madison, were beautifully shaded by a large bur oak. When the health of that tree was in doubt, it was scheduled for removal (under protest of course). Local media immediately converged on the cries that Old Abe once roosted in the tree. After the battles settled, the tree was removed and made its way to our yard. We counted rings to check the age of the tree and found the claim that it was Old Abe's roost to be unlikely. That tree was no more than a sapling in the 1860s. It turns out there is no other historical evidence to support the claim either. If there is any truth to the story, it is more likely that the bur oak limb upon which the stuffed replacement now rests is from that tree. But all that, it seems, are unimportant details. This tree has a unique history and its wood has become prized construction material for those who recall the tree for all its various memories.

**University of Wisconsin-Madison President's Oak:** This is a related story—sort of. When the Eagle Brigade formed, their gathering point and training grounds were at Camp Randall, now home to Camp Randall Stadium for the University of Wisconsin Badgers, some two miles from the State Capitol. The story is told that for training, the regiment would fire their cannons at oak trees on Observatory Hill. This all makes sense if you know the lay of the land around Camp Randall. Until recently, one tree remained on Observatory Hill from that era – the President's Oak. The tree was a badly misshapen but huge bur oak, nearly five feet across at its base. So does it look like it had been used for target practice—yes, almost certainly.

However, shortly before the Civil War broke out, the recently established university constructed its president's house only a couple hundred feet away from the tree and almost directly behind the tree from the direction of Camp Randall. So, given those added details, this particular tree was a most unlikely target for the Eagle Brigade's cannons. But who cares about those details? The tree was huge! It looked like it had been hit by a few if not several cannon balls, and that alone should make the legend stand. The president's oak also came down recently, and while no cannonballs were found, as the university's oldest and largest tree, the wood will live on.

**University of Wisconsin Memorial Union Terrace:** And now a third and more remotely connected story. If you are a University of Wisconsin Badger or alumni, I need say no more than the Memorial Union Terrace oaks. But if you have not had this privilege as part of your heritage, let me both draw and share a picture – a lakeside campus with its student union on that lake. The Terrace is a stone patio first built in 1928 as a respite between the Memorial Union and the lake. In March 1933 the Memorial Union became the first campus facility anywhere in the US to serve beer and the terrace was the place where that drink could best be savored. On a hot summer evening when a band is playing and you are sitting in a world famous sunburst terrace chair, under the shade of the huge oaks, you are in the best place in town.

UW Madison Memorial Union Terrace

If you haven't been there lately my fellow Badgers, I am sad to report that the white oak that once stood on the steps to the Union Theater came down a few years ago now. The life of that tree became a controversial preservation effort some 70 years prior as the Union Theater was being constructed a mere dozen feet away. Coincidence or not we cannot say, but the famed conservationist Aldo Leopold was a student at that time.

While the tragic news is the loss of this tree, the good news is that it moved just 60 feet south and is now the bar and drink rails in the recently restored Stiftskellar, the indoor alternative "best place" when Wisconsin's winter sets in. The terrace itself has also undergone a facelift/expansion and several additional but smaller trees from the periphery of the terrace and adjoining areas were removed and replaced. All of these trees and parts from the President's Oak are represented in a mosaic wall within the Union that will likely be revealed as this book is being printed.

And yes, the remaining large oaks are still serving their highest and best use by shading another generation of Badgers.

So here is the thing about urban wood. Even trees that are

not directly connected to a specific event may, because of location or legend, have value well beyond "normal market conditions." History is certainly worth preserving. Sometimes untrue legends are worth preserving simply because they are fun. Sometimes a welcome memory is provoked just by seeing something made from a tree that reminds you of a time. Those memories may have nothing to do with the tree that merely stood nearby at that time the memory was created, but having something that you know came from that tree suddenly becomes priceless.

    I challenge any woodlot tree or imported furniture to share the stories contained in urban wood.

# 6
# THE PLAYERS

Success of the tree to table movement involves a number of players, each with a unique set of interests that are surprisingly well suited for each other. Consider that when all of these players fit together, we are really simply restoring the woodworking economy of old. That is much of why the farm to table marketplace has moved forward so effectively; there are no losers within either a local food economy or an urban woodworking network. We will identify those involved and how they are interconnected.

**Tree Owners**

The owners of trees are, at first glance, the biggest losers in the overall tree to table movement because they are the ones losing a beloved tree. To some extent I would agree, but in reality, the loss that tree owners suffer is an unavoidable consequence of the life cycle of a tree. Trees simply don't last forever. Many of our American hardwoods span multiple human generations, so it is simply harder for us to see "grandpa's tree" reach the point of removal.

When it is time for these trees to come down, the tree to table movement provides an alternative to this "friend" simply becoming lost forever. Taking down the tree is only a short-term end point in the case of urban wood that finds its way to the urban sawyer. That tree will become one or more valued future products with a new starting point.

Tree owners are also an important partner in the tree to

table movement right from the point of planting. In those early years the owner has much to say about the survival potential and overall architecture of tree. Planting location will weigh heavily on just how large that tree can become before it becomes a problem for foundations, utilities or other urban obstacles. And once planted, the trimming that guides the young tree's growth will eventually define the overall shape of what hopefully becomes a large tree.

As mentioned previously, the urban tree is most similar to the prairie-grown tree. Low hanging limbs and double or triple trunks can usually thrive near the ground simply by growing horizontally just far enough to clear the shade line of the nearest limb on that same tree. Without the normal controls imposed by a woodlot setting, limb management and its consequences for long-term tree health fall to the owner and the skills of their arborist. Pruning for what will eventually become the major tree limbs is best done when the tree is young. Care for these younger trees is not relevant to the work of guys in this generation, but it is still the concern of future urban wood businesses.

A tree owner plays their biggest role in the current tree to table movement when making a tree removal decision. Most often a mature tree removal is only considered because of tree health or tree location. This owner is principally looking to their arborist to resolve a problem, while also dealing with the loss of a tree that most likely was valued by them. These discussions often move to what will happen to the wood. Almost as part of a grieving process, many homeowners would rather not see their tree simply become firewood and chips, yet, historically, those were the only options an arborist could offer. That may still be the common answer, but in a growing number of communities it is no longer the complete answer. Merely asking the question has opened a number of doors for dead or dying trees that have found better, more permanent and more meaningful uses. Seeking arborists that are willing to work toward these better uses helps propel the tree to table movement.

Finally, these tree owners also own the stories that give these trees part of their value. As covered previously, stories sell. I consider awareness of a tree's history to be one of those factors most important to the overall process. Often without that history the life drains out with the sap. One approach that breathes new life into a dead tree is making a project from a client's tree for that client, or at least collecting that story so it can be passed on to other future users.

**Municipalities**

We could look at municipalities as just another tree owner, but they are also the arborist and the utility manager and fill a half dozen other roles in and around those trees. We will, of course, focus on their role as the single largest tree owners/managers in most cities.

Municipalities are not only the owners and managers of sometimes substantial park lands, but they are most often the official owners for trees within street right-of-ways. Cities typically manage and trim these trees and when their removal is needed, the city or their contractor typically does the removal.

While technically owned by the city, many municipalities still recognize the tree in front of a residence is viewed by the adjoining property owner as "their tree." Although the tree may not be technically owned by them, it is certainly emotionally owned. Even if not technically included in a property sale, these trees also impact property values. A beautifully shaded street not only cools the neighborhood and shelters it from wind and street noise, it also adds an undefinable tranquility to that neighborhood.

Every time a city tree crew comes down a street, these are

the neighborhood concerns that crew needs to be prepared to address. So whether formally recognized or not, street crews commonly do what they can to accommodate those property owners (who pay the taxes that fund those street crews). Yet, these crews still need to prune and sometimes need to remove those trees. In the case of removal, it is a common practice to offer first-right-of-refusal for the log or other wood from that tree to the property owner. In some cases, this is limited to an informal "Well, we will not be back to pick it up until next Tuesday, and if it is gone by then, we don't mind."

    Municipalities also own substantial parks, land, golf courses, cemeteries and other wooded properties. Some such properties are well manicured sites, where trees are trimmed and every branch that falls is cleaned up. Other properties remain in varying degrees of more natural states, sometimes with volunteer management of invasive species or other simple improvements. Degrees of tree management in these more natural settings tend toward just keeping trails clear or minimizing liability from large hanging limbs or dead trees.

    The sheer number of trees on municipal lands is more akin to a woodlot owner than to a homeowner who might have a couple to perhaps a couple dozen trees to manage within their yard. Granted, many suburban property owners may also have an attached woodlot, but public access and management of those areas is more a question of personal preference. The municipality, however, must assume regular public access to much if not most of their wooded areas. There is also a public assumption that these trees are being managed. Picnics in the park need to occur under trees without the picnickers thinking they must first study the tree above to assess the safety of the site they choose.

    This high level of public access under and around municipal park trees, the municipal ownership of street trees and the large geographic spread of all these trees across the city landscape under limited municipal budgets creates a very unique set of circumstances. Further complicating the issue is that many of these trees are very much urban in form and require manual pruning and care to form proper structures. All the issues of urban tree architecture relate to the growth of municipal trees just as much as privately owned urban trees.

While municipalities love their shaded streets and parks and recognize their value, they are also a burden. They take time, they take equipment and they take an emotional toll. When a storm hits, municipalities take more of each than they can budget for. And even in years without severe storms, trees are still much like a pet that leaves "gifts" in the form of fall leaf cleanup.

The tree to table movement can be viewed as a friend or foe to an overstrained municipality, particularly those double-stressed by emerald ash borer issues. Yet Wisconsin Urban Wood, a non-profit organization advocating for the tree to table movement in Wisconsin, has been finding a growing number of municipal managers that are willing to adjust their operational approach in ways that improve urban wood utilization.

Those municipalities that have found success have done so through coordination with urban wood businesses to find ways that they can repurpose good logs in ways that are either cost neutral or that offer a cost savings for the municipality. The key to making this work is a joint discussion between municipal crews and wood users to evaluate processes and define methods that can make logs available without complicating the municipality's world. The overall system must also be clearly definable to the municipality's administration, legal departments and elected officials, since questions of equity will always follow.

## Arborists and Others who Cut Trees

An arborist is first of all an advocate for the tree and their owners. That is as it should be. The arborist should primarily be assessing what they can do to save the tree; perhaps pruning, perhaps reinforcing. At the bottom of the good arborist's list is removing a tree.

Others involved in tree removals might have a different view. To a utility company, trees are something that interferes with their lines, but which they can only trim so far before generating wrath from their customers. To an excavator, trees are that oversized flag attached to the root ball they need to pull out.

None of these views align with someone, like myself, who runs an urban sawmill, owns an urban lumber business and makes urban hardwood furniture, but each of these views reflect the realities of trees in an urban environment. Obviously the utility or excavator can be a log source when a removal does happen. But the arborist's interest in preserving urban trees helps to set the stage for the tree to table movement and it is the arborists who will most commonly form the best and most lasting relationship with the urban sawyer.

- First in the arborist's list of credits is the size of trees we mentioned previously. Proper management of these urban trees has resulted in so many of the champion size trees being found in urban settings. Yes, all trees have their limit, but the remarkable size of some urban logs can only be attributed to good care by both owner and arborist.
- Second is the solid structure of a well-managed urban tree. Because these urban trees tend to grow wide in addition to tall, they tend toward over-grow limbs that in a woodlot scenario would die and shed off or in a prairie setting would be trimmed

by wind. A skilled arborist assesses which limbs will help grow a strong canopy and which limbs will eventually weaken the tree if allowed to remain. Further, they are not trimming to make a tall and boring stick with leaves on top, like a woodlot tree. That is not an urban tree's primary purpose. The urban tree is intended to have some width in addition to height. It is intended to provide shade and shelter even if it is just a solo tree. This management by an arborist results in strong growth of lower limbs that, when that tree must eventually come down, will provide some amazing grain character. And yes, even those trimmed limb scars will eventually add character that you just don't find in a woodlot tree.
- Third, good arborists have a passion for trees. Like the wood craftsman, this is not a low-risk, easy-money field. It is hard work by a skilled hand with a good eye and they share this passion with their clients. They help the owner better understand the beauty, character and function of their specific trees and their words help build value into a tree for an owner who might be teetering between trimming and removing.
- Finally, the arborist is most likely to encourage replanting once a tree is lost, thus keeping the entire cycle rolling.

When I think of what makes a good arborist, the following story comes to mind.

Some time ago I had a homeowner contact me about a couple walnut trees he was thinking about having removed. I hear "big walnut" pretty often, so instead of jumping all over this, I recorded his address and gave him the names of a couple arborists in his area. Then I had a friend that knew trees and worked nearby scope it out. They mis-identified them as bur oaks. Based on the owner's description and a quick look at a marginal google map photo, that made sense. I left it at that.

A year passed and he contacted me again, this time with better pictures and measurements. He was more insistent that the nuts were driving him and his neighbors, well, nuts. For those not familiar with black walnut, a walnut with its husk is about the size of a tennis ball and the nuts can be abundant.

I checked the trees out, let him know I would be interested in the logs and again shared the name of an arborist in his immediate area who I have worked with regularly. By chance, he had just met the arborist recently.

After viewing the trees, the arborist declined to bid a removal project, but was more than happy to assist with trimming. It was not that the job was beyond his skills, I've seen him do more complex removals than this. He simply told the owner how unique his specific trees were from a size and character perspective and he assured the owner that they were in very good health. The trees still stand, at least for now. My point is simply that a good arborist will chose good advice over quick profit from a large job. That is the type of arborist you want caring for your trees and the type who I will enjoy working with on the next project.

Log economics covered in Chapter 11 will shed further light on this issue, but the simple reality is that log value is a small part of the arborist's decision making process. When the arborist does a removal, their principal cost is the skilled laborers who first assess the work, then climb, cut and lower the tree in parts without dropping those parts on the structures or utility lines below.

Once on the ground, it is those same skilled hands that transition into a brute labor force that must wrestle the heavy pieces out of a back yard. This is the part of the equation where the arborist must weigh his time against the weight of a larger log section. The extraction and subsequent transfer of a useable saw log versus shorter and more manageable firewood lengths is an intentional decision by an arborist who chooses to partner into the tree to table movement. Some are willing to engage in those additional efforts, others are not. Some of this stems from their relationship with their clients, but much of this falls to an effective working relationship with the sawyer who will pick up or receive those logs.

## Sawyers (Saw Mill Operators)

Once a removal is completed and the log transported, the urban sawmill operator is the next player on the court. More likely than not, that sawmill will fall in one of two categories — a portable band saw mill or a chain saw mill. If size permits, the sawmill operator's first choice will be a band saw mill. As mentioned in Chapter 3, the band saw is preferred over the traditional circular saw mill because it is faster, safer and cheaper to operate if there is steel, concrete or other hardware in the log. Most of these band saw mills are mobile, but in an urban setting, the more common scenario is to get the log out of the yard as quickly and efficiently as possible, then deal with sawing on a separate timeline. If the wood needs to move off-site anyway, it makes more sense to bring the log to the equipment rather than bringing the noise and dust of a mill to a neighborhood setting.

On the larger logs or branch unions where the trunk divides into two or three major limbs, a band saw may not be big enough. There are some big mills that can handle massive logs, but the price on these bigger machines requires more than occasional use and using such a mill still assumes the log can be moved to the mill. The more typical scenario is one of several varieties of mills that are essentially over-sized chain saws. Simpler units are designed to attach directly to the bar of a large chain saw, while other units include a complete framework into which the log is set and have a large customized chain saw bar attached to a power unit.

On occasion, a back yard log is simply too large to be removed as a complete log. This is where the extreme portability of a chain saw mill can come in very handy. We have pulled 3 to 4 foot wide slabs from backyards that would otherwise have become firewood because of access limitations. We have pulled 24 foot long slabs from a back yard when the longest section that could be pulled by the equipment that fit in that yard would have been a 6 foot log length.

Ideally a log is sawn very soon after being felled. In a perfect world the sawmill operator knows how the wood will be used and cuts with that end goal in mind. Contact with the tree owner that is interested in a finished product from their tree can aid this decision. Shape, size and other character traits or "defects" also drive these decisions.

To the extent the tree to table movement has a middle man, that middle man is the sawyer and kiln operator who follows. They need to coordinate with arborists, building contractors, homeowners and municipalities to accumulate the logs. Once in their yard, the sawyer also needs to know how to convert each unique log into lumber that will sell. When talking with their arborist sources, they need to be able to define what logs will align with the lumber markets they have available. Appendix A is my tool for sharing what is of greatest use for my particular marketplace.

**Kiln Operators**

In the lumber business, green is not good. Green simply refers to wood that has not yet been dried. A freshly sawn board is completely useless to the craftsman. This board contains roughly 70 percent moisture on a dry weight basis (meaning 100 pounds of dry lumber contains 70 additional pounds of water as it comes from the tree).

For use in furniture, cabinetry or flooring, the wood must be dried to roughly 8 percent moisture. Getting from one point to the other in hardwoods takes time. Time varies by species, thickness and the type of drying system used, but in general the process takes a month or longer for inch-thick lumber, two to three months for 2 inch lumber and substantially longer still for thicker lumber. Thick live-edge table slabs are best dried slowest of all; often starting with air drying, these slabs are usually cut well over a year before ready for work.

Wood drying rates must be carefully regulated to achieve the best results, and daily or near daily monitoring is part of that process, especially during the early stages of drying. Much of this is more automated in the large commercial kilns, but with their larger batch sizes, the value of personal monitoring cannot be overlooked even in the big kilns.

Most drying kilns used within the urban wood industry are smaller units that are owned and operated by the urban sawyer. These kilns may dry from several hundred to a few thousand board feet of lumber in each batch, turning green lumber with only limited uses and markets to kiln dried lumber; an in-demand useable commodity. And one final step further enhances that lumber value. Just a single pass through a planer turns the lumber from rough-sawn plank to a board that fully displays the character of the wood grain.

**Local Craftsmen**

The typical craftsman working in urban wood, at least at this point in history, is a small shop, ranging from a single, part-time hobbyist to perhaps a commercial setting of 5 to 10 employees. Economies of scale are important, since the equipment investment can range from several thousand dollars to well over $100,000, plus shop space. The hobbyist and single-person professional woodworker are both likely working from their home, where both dust and noise are constant partners. In larger cities, shared-workspace and shared equipment options are increasingly available for these smallest of businesses.

Products can range the full scope of what is possible in woods, from one-of-a-kind artistic pieces to a wide array of more traditional works. Some shops focus on a specific product line and others cover a broader range of custom products. Some produce to order, some stock inventory. Not all such shops work exclusively in urban wood, but there are certainly shops that intentionally focus efforts on this unique lumber. Even in my shop, I occasionally need to purchase lumber, since I cannot always dictate what the client will want, compared to what trees have been coming out of the local landscape. I can and do, however, decline work that is requested in woods that do not grow in my home state, but without question, taking such a stance is the exception, not the norm.

I've heard custom woodworking can be the second toughest career field to choose in life, with pastoring a church being the toughest. Neither pay well but at least the pastor has a retirement package with no expiration date. What the woodworker enjoys, however, is the ability to see the finished product during their lifetime.

Three primary challenges face the small urban wood craftsman:

- First of these is shared with the urban sawyer/kiln operator – supply and demand. To some extent, the custom woodworker dealing directly with a client can guide that client toward the urban woods that are available, but in other cases not. As mentioned above, even a shop that focuses on urban wood

might need to step into the traditional lumber market to meet the needs of specific clients.
- Second is the production process. As a smaller shop potentially competing with larger and more automated shops, each step of the process can be more time consuming. In like fashion, since urban wood tends to come with even more character, the urban wood shop may be spending more time planning their cuts around useable and non-useable parts of a board.
- And third, the finances are both different and more challenging. If the product is truly custom, each new project comes with the uncertainties of estimating time and even the uncertainty of defining client expectations. Because urban lumber generally costs more to produce and the small shop cannot purchase in wholesale quantities, the input costs are higher. And, in the end, they are competing against pricing established by a world economy. Granted, in the end, they are also producing a product with a level of craftsmanship and durability that the world economy has either forgotten or simply decides to not produce; yet the ever-present pricing of cheap and disposable furniture is always in front of the clients.

And yet these shops exist, and appear to be growing. Driven by passion or the simple desire to do what seems right, these small urban shops will continue as long as they can find clients willing to purchase their products at a price that will keep them in business.

Perhaps one other competitor should also be listed; the retiree that is willing to work for an unbelievably low hourly rate just for the joy of being in a shop. On the other hand, I will someday also "retire" and work with wood, and I already undercharge for much of my work. So let's consider the retiree an urban woodworking partner instead of a competitor.

## The Client Base

The client is what makes the whole system work. From the point that myself and others like me started trying to organize our efforts in Wisconsin, we have continually pointed to the client or more generally the marketplace as the key to the urban wood industry. As long as trees grow in cities, there will be arborists to maintain them and eventually to cut them down. If there is a market for urban lumber, sawyers will saw and kilns will dry. But the whole system relies on clients willing to purchase products made from local, urban wood. American industry has a great ability to meet demand.

The client base does exist, so for those of you, thanks. From my experience as a functioning urban wood business for more than 15 years now, people are interested in the wood that grows around them. At first I thought this might just be a Madison thing, but as many other businesses have been springing up across the nation, we can definitely conclude it is far from just a local phenomenon.

If anything, the limiting factor is awareness. The world economy has successfully trained people to assume the local craftsman no longer exists. The world economy has also successfully trained people into thinking local wood no longer exists. Where does wood come from anyway? We know we can get a 2x4 at the local big box lumber store, but we know it comes from somewhere far away by the semi load. We can also find oak and perhaps a couple other excessively common hardwood species as pre-sized lumber or pre-milled trim. They may even have a couple premium hardwood species shrink wrapped in one of three convenient sizes; again all delivered by a semi from somewhere far away.

Many larger towns also have a specialty tool store that offers good quality hardwoods, but ask the check-out staff where that wood comes from and you may get a blank stare. Fewer people know where to find other hardwoods, or particularly where to find character wood.

The tree to table movement grows with awareness. Let's face it, why am I, as an urban woodworker, writing this book, but to further its growth? Yes, urban wood is a smart thing to do. It meets all the green, sustainable, local and low input trigger points we can think of. But it also makes good business sense for me to tell people what my colleagues and I are doing. This book just simplifies the process in many regards. I have these discussions about what I do almost daily; why not find a more efficient means of sharing this incredibly efficient woodworking option?

So when I talk about urban wood I like to circle back to the tree owners. These are after all the folks that start the whole urban wood cycle. These are also often the most impassioned clients, since they know the tree's history and may be responsible for some of the character that appears in the lumber. Every time I meet a homeowner at a tree removal, I ask whether they have considered having something made from the tree. Surprisingly, many people who call me because they don't want the wood from their tree to be wasted have not considered that they could also use the wood for furnishing their home. Some wonderful designs have come from these discussions.

## Organizations

This is the newest addition to the tree to table movement. Back in the first chapter I shared some stories from my youth regarding lumber that would now be classified as urban lumber, but I am by no means the first to use urban lumber. Many small shops have been doing this for years. I still remember each time I learned about another shop doing work like myself, each one providing additional assurance that my thought process was somewhat sane.

The reality for myself or any other small shop, is that there is never much time to go beyond the next few projects or beyond the confines of your existing local connections to see what is going on in the next city over.

    This is where we come back to emerald ash borer and the sudden need to start asking these questions. This is where the short-term window of state and federal grants aimed at urban wood problems and potential solutions has come in helpful. Most of the coordinating efforts and infrastructure development that is occurring at this time are a result of various forms of EAB or urban forest management grants. These organizational efforts are allowing individual shops to connect with each other and share both common and unique resources and experiences. These organizations can also explore public outreach opportunities that may be beyond the potential of any individual business.

    Under the client base heading above we mentioned that the tree to table industry can build all the components needed to bring the movement along at whatever pace a client base is built. The free enterprise system is excellent at this process. The key role that organizations are playing is building awareness that the concept is even possible. Those of us already established in this industry have seen the public is interested; they are just largely unaware of the options and individual small businesses have a hard time sharing that option to a broader waiting audience.

    Essentially the tree to table movement is rising out of the woodwork by organizing. Municipalities across the eastern half of the U.S. have a vested interest in the options because of what emerald ash borer is doing to their neighborhoods, but only for a short window of time. It is during this time that both the public and private sectors are motivated to find ways to work together, both to solve local problems and simultaneously build their local economies. The public funding will likely wither as the ash trees do. But, again, that little bug has provided an opportunity to build awareness of urban lumber's potential and that awareness can have a lasting impact with those communities.

# 7
# TIMELINES

Close to 20 years ago now, I met a Windsor chair maker who once boasted fairly regular work on a fairly regular basis. Then word got out and he moved from a sometimes backlog to a three-month backlog, and then six months. By this point he was concerned that the backlog might hurt his business, but he did not want to hire a crew, yet, you cannot say "no" to a wanting client.

As it turned out, his fear and his observations differed. What he thought would be "Oh, I'm not waiting that long" became "Oh, we better get our order in right away." His backlog stabilized at around nine months and stayed there for several years.

A nine-month backlog is not normal, and certainly not since 2009. That is not the timeline of the tree to table movement. More than anything, this movement is just a new (and simultaneously ancient) way of doing business. In most cases we are not adding anything to the process; instead we are subtracting the excessive transportation steps of the world economy.

The reality is the local craftsman doing what they do best still competes well on a timeline basis. "Just-in-time delivery" within the global market really means the store nearest to you doesn't carry a full inventory of what could be made, they just have as many options as they feel are necessary. Interestingly, this also comes with a side benefit for them. They know they can produce additional sizes and just call them custom orders. Doesn't "custom order" sound more impressive, even if their "custom" only means a choice between a limited number of pre-defined parameters? For the urban wood craftsman, it is not a cookie-cutter, throw it together approach. A person going to a store and ordering a factory-produced furniture piece in a "customized" size or color is commonly told four to six weeks, or depending upon what continent it originates from, eight to ten weeks. The local craftsman can do that and so much more.

This really puts the local custom craftsman of the tree to table movement into perspective. Again, the true shift of the tree to table movement is really a way of doing business and a decision to source locally. Only in some more limited cases, which we will discuss, is it slower than the ordering a factory-produced furniture piece

To grasp a better understanding, let us consider the parallel of the tree to table movement – the farm to table movement, which has also been nicknamed the slow food movement. "Slow food" really says nothing about a timeline, it is instead more of a subtle rebellion to "fast food," which has become so institutionally uniform that it looks, smells and tastes the same anywhere on the planet. Fast food is predictable, but it also introduces an institutional feel and taste to eating.

So, in an era where speed and efficiency is so important, why do we see restaurants springing up that not only offer, but flaunt a menu based on locally grown produce? Their menus are so unpredictable that – get this – it varies by what is available within the confines of the local agricultural season. That's crazy from a business standpoint, and yet it is exactly what we want.

We want to know where our food came from, who produced it, and what efforts they went through to get it to us. We want to know everything about it, and we are willing to sit down and wait for it to show up on our plates just to experience the story. What is dining, after all, if not simply slowing down the food consumption process to the benefit of all?

Are we getting the point? Urban woodworking, or tree to table, is just the same but in a more lasting medium. And, getting back to timelines, the actual time spent preparing a fast food meal compared to a farm to table "slow" food meal is not that much different. It's more a question of what the chef has to work with and what flexibility he is granted to adjust the menu or the preparation of an individual plate. Likewise, the tree to table craftsman works with whatever their local urban landscape offers. The tree to table craftsman is also cognizant of how they can best utilize these local offerings in a manner that pleases their clientele. Sometimes those offerings are as local as your own backyard. Regardless, if you participate in the tree to table movement, you will be well fed with stories, and unique flavors that the "fast wood" economy will not offer.

Having said all this, there is one scenario where we do need to specifically discuss the timeline, and that is in dealing with wood drying. Whether for urban hardwoods or for the commercial lumber industry, wood drying is the slowest step in the processing sequence. Drying times play such a significant factor in scheduling a project that we really need to describe the two most common scenarios separately – already dried lumber versus green logs.

**Already Dried Lumber**

This is the more common scenario for the urban wood craftsman. If the wood is dry, we are primarily talking about a scheduling question.

The commercial factory can move a project through their factory faster than a fine craftsman can through a small shop, but that is only part of the equation. If that shop is not local, you need move paperwork and specifications through the system, then have the design department check things over to make sure all the options are standard, or schedule a designer to detail anything that is truly custom. If the work is truly custom, you may also need to call up the supply chain and factor in their shipping schedules before even putting it on the production schedule. Once built and finished it still needs to go back through the wholesale/retail distribution system before it is available. Each person with their work backlog and scheduling parameters means four to six weeks is generally considered a quick turn-around, even though the in-shop production itself may be a question of hours or days.

Compare this with the small local shop with its slightly slower equipment. Likely the design department and the production system are different lobes in the same mind or at most two guys that talk face-to-face throughout the day. Both shops can be busy, but a four to six week timeline does not mean four to six weeks in the shop for either person. Hopefully those of us who know what we are doing are good enough to estimate our timeline and deliver on schedule, which after all is the most important aspect of a timeline. I've certainly had projects where I've fallen off my target timeline and needed to adjust, but if the lumber is dry, the primary question for large or small shop is scheduling, not actual production speed.

Working with urban wood just adds one additional detail to the puzzle. The primary question is really more a question of wood availability than one of production rate. My shop runs a sawmill and kiln, and we both sell lumber locally and build with it in our own shop. So it seems like having the right wood available at the right time should be easy. But this is the true test of real custom woodworking.

Having all the right woods in all the right thicknesses, widths and lengths is not so easy. I have 30 bins in one storage area where I try to keep as many species and thicknesses available and accessible as possible, but in those 30 bins I just have the four most common thicknesses for seven species, with only a couple bins to spare. The bins are handy, but based on trees recently removed from the local urban landscape, I currently have 15 species in stock with as many as six thicknesses in some species. We have not even begun to discuss lumber grades, cutting methods and other character sorting criteria that could further multiply the needed bin counts.

Frankly, we sometimes carry more of an inventory than we should just to protect ourselves from running out of what the next client may request. This past year my weak link was 3-inch thick walnut. I had it, but everything I had was big live edge slabs and I needed table leg stock for another big slab that was being made into a table. The solution was painful but possible; cut a big slab into legs. Finding the right urban wood is less like picking up a standard stick at a lumber yard, and more comparable to a woodworker's search for a specific imported exotic. Much of this goes well beyond what they typical factory shop will even offer.

For those who don't run their own lumber business, finding the right wood already dry and locally available is a much bigger consideration than our big-mill conventional lumber counterparts face. We are, after all, not sawing based on a supply and demand system, but are instead sawing based on availability and continually seeing what we can do to adjust demand to match supply.

Before offering a project in urban wood, the craftsman must be tuned into what grows in the area and what urban mills in the area may have available. Often the client has a "look" in mind more than they have a specific wood species in mind. If the craftsman can grasp that look, then they may have the freedom to alert the client on a local wood that might serve that function and provide the desired look.

Ash, for example, has a traditional nickname of poor man's oak. This really is an undeserved title since the quality of the wood does stand alone and it has character traits that are unique. At the same time, if ash and oak are stained similarly, many people would not notice the difference unless it was specifically pointed out, simply because the grain is similar when stained.

The craftsman just needs to check before they bid. Local mills may have it, but only in certain thicknesses. Or they may just have logs they have not sawn yet, and therefore the wood will also need to dry in the kiln for two to four months. I've given out all these answers to callers; both clients and those within my urban wood network. These answers may not result in a no, it may simply change the scheduling. I have on several occasions been able to sell wood even before it goes into the kiln. Without question, if I have a kiln backlog and I know pile A is sold as soon as it is dry and pile B is just building inventory, I will find a way to get pile A dried as quickly as the wood fibers will permit.

If the timeline or availability doesn't line up, but the customer is truly interested in urban wood, there is almost always a workable option. I once did a kitchen where, honestly, their first question about wood was, "What do you have for local woods?" My answer, "Well, I have enough hackberry from a tree that grew five blocks up the street." Who in their right mind would think to bid a kitchen in hackberry? I know I wouldn't have if I didn't have it dried and ready to go. But this half-joking remark resulted in probably the first hackberry kitchen in town, and it looks outstanding. I learned something important that day.

Maybe a year after the hackberry incident, I had a client tell me they kind of liked the character of oak, but wanted something a little different. I was sitting on 1,200 board feet of black locust that was just recently dried, but with no plans. I decided to try the hackberry experiment again. I prepared a sample and they now have a black locust kitchen. Before I was done with that kitchen a client came into the shop and asked what kind of wood it was – that lead to a second black locust kitchen. By the third request I was out of locust, so that couple decided to postpone their remodel until I next got enough black locust to do their kitchen. I've done four now.

The nice side of supply and demand is that it tends to work out, even in urban wood. In the Midwest, the most abundant trees in our landscape are also those that we are asked about most often: cherry, walnut, red oak, and white oak big enough for quarter sawing, maple, hickory and a few others. Because local preferences reflect what was historically used in the area, this same principal occurs elsewhere. These requests only get skewed by marketing efforts that bring lesser known woods into an area, often because they are cheaper. The Midwest is currently seeing this with alder; a wood I've heard described as the west coast weed tree. Perhaps we should start shipping boxelder to the west coast and then use our own urban wood to provide a whole new lineup of "exotics" to the craftsman's pallet on those projects where they can guide the species selection.

As the tree to table movement grows, networking also grows. Those of us on the lumber production side of the Wisconsin Urban Wood network are regularly checking in with each other to see what is available.

I just got a call from another urban lumber dealer to let me know that for a short time he has access to a truckload quantity of urban ash. Once it is gone, he does not know when he will next have that large of quantity available again. I recently sent out word through the network that I was looking for black locust, which one of the guys happened to have available and a third partner was a couple boards short on walnut, while I had plenty of in stock.

In theory, we are all competitors, but we also recognize each other as partners. These same networking scenarios certainly happen in the traditional lumber markets, but on a much larger scale and on more readily available species. If something is in short supply, there are plenty of woodlot trees of that species waiting. Urban wood is a little less predictable, so the networking becomes more essential and personal.

**Logs or Green Lumber to Finished Projects**

We probably need to start this section with yet another definition; green lumber?

We are not talking about green treated lumber in the racks at the local building materials store. Neither are we talking about wood grown in a more sustainable manner. We are simply talking about moisture. Logs or lumber that still has an elevated moisture content from while it was growing is known as green lumber. A typical hardwood contains 60 to 70 percent moisture while growing, yet as furniture, cabinetry or flooring, that lumber must be reduced to approximately 8 percent moisture.

As an interesting side note: calling an unseasoned employee "green" comes from woodworking, in fact "unseasoned" itself is a wood drying term.

Working from logs or green lumber is where the scheduling stretches longer. Drying hardwoods is and must be a slow process in order to achieve good results. If you rush the process you wreck the wood. Typical drying technology used for urban wood will require four to six weeks drying time for inch thick lumber (known as 4/4 or four quarter, meaning the rough sawn boards are four quarters of an inch thick). Six quarter (1.5-inch thick lumber) may take six to eight weeks and eight quarter lumber will likely take 10-12 weeks.

Of the more common hardwoods, oak is on the slowest end of the spectrum, while ash, cherry, walnut and several others are on the faster end of the spectrum. Very thick and wide live edge slabs are on the extreme end of the spectrum. These are so far out that the world experts in wood drying, the U.S. Forest Products Research Service, do not even offer drying schedules for this wood. Based on our experience, I follow a year-long drying process.

So why would we design with wood that is not even dry yet? Why not? Does a builder when specifying a trim package know where that wood is? No, they likely never ask that question and are likely unaware that the wood they will eventually use likely sits as a log in some yard if not still a tree in some woodlot at the time they are signing contracts. They are simply specifying something that they can predict the price of and know they can get at the drop of a hat. And yet, most times I've had this discussion with a builder, they are very skeptical that the wood from their own jobsite could ever be ready in time for the project.

Waiting for wood to dry does not make a project infeasible. Consider that a log can be sawn within the week, if not the same day that the tree is felled. Add five weeks drying time and you could be working on wood from that tree within six weeks. Millwork or flooring could be processed and ready for installation within another week. I don't typically tell my clients that I will have their wood ready for them in six to eight weeks because of my own work schedules, but if intentionally scheduled for a fast turn-around we can typically accomplish just that.

Based on these timelines, we can usually use trees removed from a construction site in the construction project itself. For instance, if a homeowner is adding on but needs to take a tree down to make room for the expansion, we can have the tree sawn and dried in time to use the wood for trim, flooring or cabinetry in that project.

In these cases, the home owner, without a doubt, thought long and hard about the tree or trees that needed to be removed for their project. How better to relieve concern over the tree removal than incorporating the tree into the project? We've done a number of projects where the trees that stood where the addition or new house was built became the trim or flooring for that house. We are currently harvesting several cherry trees from a building site that will be going back into that home as both flooring and trim.

My standing question to any homeowner I talk with about a tree scheduled for removal is whether they are interested in having something made from the tree. Normally, the owner has not thought that far ahead. They know the tree must come out and have gone through all the thought processes related to that, but rarely have they connected what must happen outside their walls with what could happen inside their walls. Even folks who don't want to see their tree become firewood often haven't connected that the beloved tree could simply move inside.

Usually if a tree is considered for future furniture purposes, the timeline of drying is even less of an impediment. The tree removal is often an unplanned expense. I have found future clients to be somewhat relieved that an immediate decision on making furniture from their tree is not necessary. I do typically want to get them thinking so that we have an idea of how we might cut the log, but the log can also sit months before we need to saw it and a year or more before we really need to nail down a final decision and the details related to using that wood. The true deadline is more a matter of how long we are willing to store the lumber.

The drying timeline is significant in a broader sense when considering wood not yet sawn. If we know that we will not be getting to a project for some time, wood can be specifically sawn to our needs. We regularly cut logs to specific thicknesses and widths for projects that will be happening in our shop or for other woodworkers we saw for. Sawing to the needs of a specific client can be good not only for the woodworker, but also for the sawyer.

Sawing for a specific project or specific client request sure beats guessing what thicknesses and widths might be needed or might sell best.

In the end, the tree to table timeline is a combined question of lumber inventory, lumber moisture and work scheduling. I run my own sawmill and sit on a sizable inventory, so if we or our custom woodworking clients are just talking about making a project from urban wood that is already dried inventory, the answer is just a question of where the project will fit in the shop schedule. If we are working with their fresh cut log, we can almost always figure out a schedule that works within the client's and builder's timeline.

# 8
# KNOW YOUR CUTS;
# HOW A SAWYER SEES A TREE

A sawyer, a person who saws logs into lumber, looks at a tree differently. To sawyers, trees are logs on the hoof – a living version of something they might someday bite into. This is not to say they do not appreciate trees as trees, but their mind does not stop there. Just like the dermatologist who may be off the clock and walking through a mall when they see an unusual skin condition and almost sub-consciously start diagnosing the cause. Or the mechanic who hears a ticking sound as a car drives by and instantly concludes that car will be in the shop for a specific repair within the next week.

Many of us never really turn off during our down time, and this is especially true for certain creative personalities who are forever being inspired by their surroundings. I once saw a repair on a wood sculpture as I walked past it at an art show. The sculpture stood more than six feet tall and the repair was no more than a half inch across. To the sculptor it was a repair, but for me it was the inspiration for the design of several furniture pieces I have made. You could place that sculpture side by side with my furniture pieces and likely no one but myself would see any correlation.

For the sawyer who is also a woodworker or wood artist, analyzing a tree becomes even more complex. Different shapes and sizes all conjure up images of what is inside that tree and how one could best exhibit the amazing character so that others can appreciate what they already see. There are several standing and healthy trees that, when I look at them, I visualize completed pieces of furniture. Likewise, there are pieces of furniture that I can visualize, however, I have yet to find the tree to make it happen; or at least no tree scheduled for removal. There is probably a name for this affliction, but those of us with it are not seeking a cure.

The sawyer also looks at a circle and sees a square. This is not part of their affliction – it is part of their skill. Setting the log on the mill and positioning it for that first cut is no small decision because the first cut largely determines what is possible from the entire log. The placement of the log for the first cut will determine the four faces of every subsequent board. The sawyer must still decide from which side of the log each subsequent board will be cut, but that first cut defines the four faces from which they will work.

As that first slab is removed, the history of the tree's growth is revealed. Each line of the grain reveals a year of that tree's life. This history is even more significant within urban trees. Each line of grain points back to stories that occurred in, under or around that tree. The sawyer is both the first to see this and the one who determines how those stories are best extracted from the tree. The furniture client is as dependent upon the sawyer's eye as they are on the craftsman's hand.

Within the commercial logging and lumber markets there are differing grades of logs and differing grades of lumber. There are a number of log grading approaches, but the photo below shows representative high and low grade logs within the USDA log grading rules. These rules assess a log's potential based on those factors that most impact what can be sawn from the log, both in quality and quantity. The principal defects that reduce the value of a log are small size, knots (or former tree limbs), crooks, cracks and decay. A good log will have less of these factors evident on the sides and ends of the log.

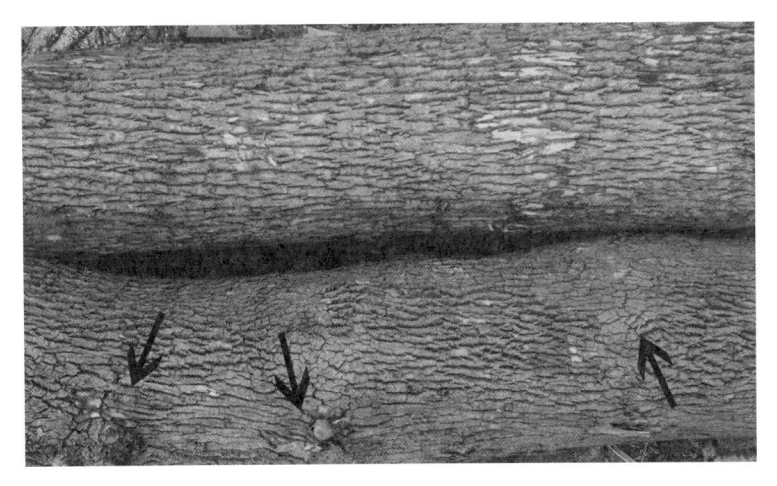

Top Log: Grade 1 Ash | Bottom Log: Grade 3 Ash with crook and limb scars noted

    The best of the best logs head for a veneer market, where they will be thinly sliced and laid on a substrate of lower value lumber veneers or compressed wood fibers. The generic name is plywood, but high quality hardwoods are sometimes laid up on other substrate materials. These veneers may be as thin as 1/64th to 1/100th of an inch in thickness, so the character of nearly every fiber of that log will become visible in its end use. Even fine woodworkers who prefer working in solid stock over veneer cannot dismiss that veneer has its place in the world of fine woodworking and that some logs could or arguably should go to a veneer mill. Yet, because of hardware within trees and the high cost of the incredibly sharp knives that cut veneer, urban logs are rarely considered viable veneer candidates.

    The balance of the top grading logs are the best saw logs; logs destined to become conventional lumber. Sometimes even logs that would be great veneer candidates are left for sawing because of demand or other circumstances. Other logs in this grade are just somewhere less than perfect, perhaps with defects limited to one side of the log or near the ends of the logs. Perhaps the log has an irregularity in the bark that points to lumber characteristics making it less than ideal for veneer. Perhaps there are some bumps that are evidence of long-healed limb scars, recognized by both logger and sawyer as a knot. Perhaps there are one or more fracture lines, worm holes, discoloration or decay in the end of the log, or simply a curve over its length. These logs may yield many large clear boards, but just do not quite offer veneer potential. These logs are most often the first length off the stump (a butt log). Yet in a woodlot setting a tree may yield this high quality for 10 to more than 40 feet up the tree before increasing crooks, knots or diameter, which brings the log grade down.

    A good sawlog will be no less than 8 feet-3 inches long and even the smaller portable mills used by urban sawyers are designed with this length in mind. Yes, shorter lumber can be sawn, but in the commercial hardwood lumber industry, 8 feet 3 inches to 16 feet 8 inches are the "normal" log lengths.

    The top grade logs are determined based on viewing a log as if it had four faces, with the grade assigned based on the second worst face. Commercial log values are based on the both the log size and quality. So, as inefficient as it may seem, if cutting a couple feet off a log improves the quality enough to offset the smaller size, that shorter log may still have a higher market value. So the end is dropped and left in the woods. In an urban setting, there is no reason to cut off minor defects. The arborist will simply leave the log as large as they can pull it from the yard and be done. The sawyer is simply going to look at what arrives and saw whatever is useable, so the only trimming is what they conclude is completely unusable.

    The next lower grades within the realm of log quality are logs that may still be sawn for lumber, but will yield a lower percentage of good lumber. As a general rule, the highest grade logs produce more than 60 percent of their lumber in the upper two lumber grades discussed below (FAS & No.1), mid-grade logs generally produce between 40 percent and 60 percent in those top lumber grades, and the bottom grade logs generally produce less than 40 percent of their yield as higher grade lumber. The lesser lumber will be used for flooring, pallets or other markets where knots, fractures and even minimal levels of decay will not be a problem or can be cut out and discarded. Often the entire low grade log heads to those aimed at this market and the fewer good boards may be pulled or left in the production line for these uses.

Lumber from Grade 1 Log
(few knots)

Lumber from Grade 3 Log
(many and larger knots)

While high-grade logs are found in the urban landscape, they are less abundant because of the commonly shorter trunks found in urban trees and the limitations on what can be pulled from back yards with smaller arborist-scaled equipment. These trees are often being removed for health reasons, so decay and fractures are more common. All of this creates additional challenges for the urban sawyer, but also offers opportunities.

The urban sawmill works with what the landscape provides and is willing to provide their clients with cuts of lumber that the commercial market does not consider worthy of uses other than flooring or pallets. And for a high-production mill, they are right to do so. Pulling three to a dozen boards aside because they offer something unique, and then trying to find that unique client is highly inefficient for a mill that runs millions of board feet per year and sees more than a thousand individual pieces each workday.

Below this, but still within the log realm, are cull logs or pulpwood. Pulpwood is typically the lowest grade of wood that is still worthy of being pulled from a woodlot, but only if there is enough to justify a trip to a paper mill. Depending upon distance, this certainly means no less than a semi load of logs, and could mean a minimum of multiple truck loads or rail car loads. Species can also be a significant factor at this level, since different paper mills want only specific species for their various product lines.

In an urban setting, pulpwood is rarely an option. Without substantial consolidation and sorting yards there are too many species and too low of volume, all of which become impractical given the market value of pulp wood. Firewood is the urban equivalent of pulpwood and this is also a good use for wood that is available because it must be removed, but is not viable for lumber.

And still one more log 'grade' exists within the urban realm that does not exist in the woodlot setting – chips. Tree-top brush and smaller limbs are typically chipped and find a number of potential uses from mulch to energy production to animal bedding. Both this wood and the firewood above are valuable components of the urban tree, but are not components that are within the focus of this book.

By the necessity of their chosen path, the urban sawyer is willing to accept lesser logs, but they also need to draw a line in the sawdust as to what they are typically willing to accept. We will further discuss the scope of what comes from their sawing, but the appendix to this book has served my business well in drawing that line as to what logs are most worthy of attention, based on Midwestern tree species and our lumber marketplace as we further describe later. Since differing species grow to differing sizes and serve differing purposes, this list reflects what we have found available and most useable, both in diameter and lengths. Will we saw lesser logs? Yes, either upon request for a specific client, especially if they want something made from their log, or if we find our inventory low on a specific wood that we desire. For the convenience of an arborist making a delivery, we also sometimes accept "ride-along" logs that are smaller but easier to drop at one destination than at multiple locations. These might also be sawn just because they are here.

This may seem counter-intuitive, but in the appendix listing you will also note there are some logs that we might decline because of excessive size, such as silver maple. Those declines are based on milling capacity and market demand. Larger logs require a slower sawing system for our business and that slower system does not make sense on species where their inherent market value drops below the cost of sawing and drying, all based on our local supply and demand. In most cases, there are plenty of ideally-sized logs to meet local demand.

**Lumber Grades**

As hinted above, log grades are simply a reflection of what can be anticipated for lumber from that log. The lumber industry has well-established standards for lumber quality. Any specific pass of the sawmill can reveal a multitude of "defects," with that term pointing to a set of character traits that make a board different than what is normal for that species. All trees can have knots, cracks, rot and a number of other traits that disrupt the normal pattern of grain. In an economy that primarily produces products without a known end client, unpredictable grain patterns are bad. Lumber grading standards are a very useful tool to help defined 'normal.' Grades are regularly used to help a client better understand or select a specific look.

The National Hardwood Lumber Association (NHLA) is the official keeper of American hardwood lumber grading standards. There are general standards that apply across essentially all species, then specific standards that apply to several specific species where the normal standards are not a good fit, or where history has assigned certain quality aspects to differing parts of the tree.

For example, the yellow birch tree's heartwood (center of the log) and the sapwood (perimeter of the log) are different colors. Those parts of the tree are often marketed separately as red birch (heartwood) and white birch (sapwood). Differing cuts from a tree may also be priced separately, (such as plain-sawn and quarter-sawn) and unique character traits are recognized in some boards (such as curly or birdseye). Much of these commonly recognized details are maintained by NHLA.

The highest grade of lumber within the NHLA standards is FAS, followed by Select, No.1 Common, No.2 Common and No. 3 Common, with additional subdivisions within these grades. In highly over-simplified terms, a FAS board will yield more than 83 percent or 10/12th of the worst face of the board in defect-free areas with defined minimum dimensions. A No. 3 Common board may yield as little as 33 percent or 4/12th of its face in defect-free areas of smaller sizes.

# KNOW YOUR CUTS; HOW A SAWYER SEES A TREE | 117

Photos of FAS, No.1 and No.3 boards; based on knots alone. (top to bottom)

Grade logically determines market value. Wood with fewer defects yield more useable material in larger individual cuttings and it also means the user spends less time cutting around defects. For this reason, a wide board with defects toward one edge is typically trimmed narrower so the high-grade section can be sold for its higher value and only the area with knots is sold for the lower value or discarded.

And regardless of the grade of a log, that log will yield varying grades of lumber. Obviously a higher grade log will yield a higher percentage of better lumber, but not exclusively. The center area of a log represents the early growth of a tree, commonly known as juvenile wood. Juvenile wood tends to be weaker wood, with fractures and multiple knots from early limbs. Quality of this inner portion of the tree is so suspect that this area is disregarded in log grading. In species where sapwood is generally considered less desirable, the outer one to three inches of the log may also be considered less valuable because of that sapwood. The best wood is generally found between the juvenile growth and the sapwood.

In a production system that handles literally millions of board feet per year, tracking of individual logs or which board came from which tree is irrelevant. Yes, this happens on the highest value veneer logs, but not the log that is sawn to lumber. Lumber is not sorted by log, but by grade, length and any other predefined criteria into which large lots can be grouped and sold.

An alternative approach to individually graded boards are two additional but seldom used standards within the National Hardwood Lumber Association rules – "log run" and "mill run." Log run includes all boards cut from a log, ranging from FAS to No.2 Common. Mill run likewise includes all boards cut from a log, but ranging down to No.3 Common. These categories will likely result in wider boards, but would not be a sawmill's first choice when dealing with higher quality logs, since this cutting strategy would not be to their economic gain unless they have a specific market for this random mix of lumber. These criteria become important, however to the urban wood marketplace.

Taking this one step further, some urban sawyers also offer flitch sawn lumber. A flitch refers to sequential slices from the same log and sometimes logs are specifically sawn and tracked or numbered in a sequential order, so that the woodworker can purchase only wood from a specific tree, or intentionally sequence slabs of wood from that tree. This is particularly common in live edge lumber described in the next chapter.

**The Special Case of Black Walnut**

Walnut is always used as the high-value extreme for American hardwoods. There are "domestic exotic" woods that can compare or exceed walnut, such as birdseye maple or curly cherry. But for conventional lumber species, walnut is always at the top of the pricing range, even without special grain patterns (figure). Just the normal grain patterns of walnut are wonderful, the natural coloring is intense and the wood is very workable in both the shop and the finish room.

Walnut has long been used for everything from fine furniture to barn construction. It was also the wood of choice for gunstocks. In fact, after two world wars, the nation's walnut supply was decimated. I remember an aging farmer from my hometown sharing that, as a youth, he remembers government staff coming to the family farm searching out walnut for the war effort. He recounted his father being told which trees they would be taking and what they would be paid for those trees. While they supported the war effort, they did not appreciate the approach the government took in collecting these trees. Nor did they appreciate the loss of the wood – farmers had come to depended on walnut for fencing, hay racks and other farm construction. We are now a full tree-generation past the world wars and as the supply of walnut grows, so does its popularity. As always, walnut is holding its value well.

Throughout our current generations, most people familiar with walnut are familiar with its potential value. As a result, the trees were left to grow – whether they were growing in a woodlot or a backyard. When they needed to come down, the local farmer sawmill network stepped into action and the lumber was stacked in a hay mow for later use or sale. To this day, here in the Midwest, we regularly find piles of walnut lumber in haylofts that suddenly reemerge at farm auctions or as these old barns are torn down.

Much of the world's black walnut supply starts on farms of the American Midwest. Woodlot harvests are scheduled as trees meet sufficient size or as the regular swings in the farm economy dictate the need for additional cash flow from this slowly maturing crop. Under this system, most commercially harvested walnut is 16 to 24 inches in diameter.

Larger walnuts are uncommon. I personally have never seen a walnut greater than 30 inches in diameter at chest height in a woodlot. They exist, but they are extremely rare. A large woodlot walnut is carefully watched because of its potential veneer value. At some point, the landowner must make the call as to whether it is best to get another year of growth on their tree, at the risk of losing that tree to a thunderstorm, a lightning strike, tornado or to the woodlot equivalent of cattle rustling – a walnut tree theft.

Because of the high value of walnut, and especially the value of walnut veneer logs, the National Harwood Lumber Association has different grading standards for walnut. Grades largely assume that the best veneer logs are not available for sawn lumber production system, so from those logs that remain, the sawn lumber has several relaxed standards for walnut. This table shows the differences for sizes.

## FAS Lumber Grade Standards (Size criteria only)

|  | Minimum Board Size | Minimum Defect Free Area Sizes |
| --- | --- | --- |
| Standard for Most Hardwoods (Oak, Maple, Cherry, etc.) | 6 inches wide 8 feet long | 4 inches wide by 5 feet long OR 3 inches wide by 7 feet long |
| Standard for Black Walnut | 5 inches wide 6 feet long | 4 inches wide by 3 feet long OR 3 inches wide by 6 feet long |

There are additional differences, but these are all reflections of the industry being willing to reflect the value of certain lumber in grade considerations, under the assumption that fewer high-grade walnut logs are available for lumber.

Walnut is also a wood where the blonde sapwood of the tree has traditionally been a non-preferred part of the tree. Sapwood is such a significant factor in the commercial walnut market that grading standards specifically address acceptable levels of sapwood within each grade level. On an FAS board, for example, both faces are limited to 1/6th of the surface measure in sapwood on boards that are five to seven inches wide, and less than 1/4 of the surface area in sapwood on a board measuring over eight inches wide.

Interestingly, the industry learned that the sapwood of walnut will transition from blonde to a grayish brown if heated while the wood is still green. This is typically accomplished by injecting steam into a chamber filled with logs or tightly stacked green sawn lumber before the drying process is started. While the coloring of heartwood and sapwood remains distinguishable in steamed walnut, the difference is so substantially reduced that the grading restrictions for steamed walnut eliminates the sapwood restrictions. Because of this, essentially all larger mill and kiln operations steam their walnut lumber. The same holds true with cherry, which also has the heartwood/sapwood color contrast, with the sapwood being traditionally less preferred and where steam can lessen the contrast.

At the same time, a growing percentage of woodworkers and their customers appreciate the contrast of heartwood and sapwood colors in woods such as walnut and cherry. Many of those seeking walnut with its natural color mix would also argue that steam reduces color intensity and variation within the heartwood. Given the predominance of steaming in the larger commercial sector, small mills and kilns are the best source for walnut that has its full range of natural colors.

## Sawing Strategies

How a log is sawn can also dictate value beyond the simple grading standards. Most notably is quartersawing lumber. The term quartersawing goes back to an era when logs were sometimes so big, the only way to saw that log was to cut it lengthwise into quarters then saw each quarter separately.

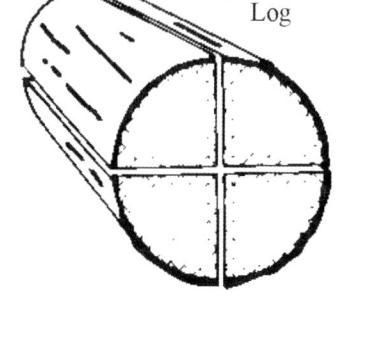

Quatersawn Log

Quartersawing is in contrast to a normal log, where boards are cut from the four sides of a squared-up log, also called a cant. Under this approach, which is the standard method used for almost all lumber, the sawyer simply looks at what side of the log will produce the best lumber and makes their cuts from that face until another side will produce better boards, again based on the defects and grading criteria described above. In this sketch, the lumber is considered plain sawn.

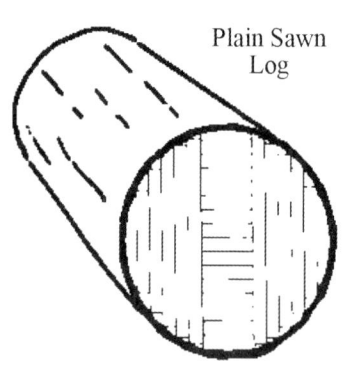

Plain Sawn Log

Other than just the size of what fits on the mill, there are other important differences between these two sawing strategies. First is that quartersawn lumber tends to dry flatter and move less with seasonal moisture changes over the life of the finish product. This was particularly important prior to the era of kiln drying. Before drying kilns, a woodworker could not reach a point dry enough to assure their work would not warped or mis-shape the finished product. Stability is one reason why many antiques were produced with quartersawn lumber. In fact, I challenge my readers to find a single pre-1900s antique oak furniture piece that is not quartersawn.

With kiln drying now standard practice on hardwoods, the more significant distinction between plain sawn and quartersawn strategies is the look of the resulting boards. In a plain sawn board, every slight irregularity in the shape of a log is amplified by cutting at an angle across the annual growth rings of the tree, resulting in more variable grain patterns within each board and across each board. Generally, the edges of the boards have straighter lengthwise grain lines and the centers of the boards have more swirling or arched grain patterns, commonly called cathedral grain.

Plain Sawn (Top) | Quatersawn (Bottom) ; both with grain enhanced

Quartersawn lumber is cut close to if not directly perpendicular to the annual rings of the tree. The grain patterns are far straighter and narrower; since it is essentially just the thickness of what was grown each year. These straight line grain patterns became particularly significant to the Arts and Crafts design era.

Depending upon the tree species, there is also a second level of grain within the tree that only appears in the quartersawn lumber. This is grain that grows from the center of the log toward the outside, rather than along the length of the log. This secondary grain is called medullary rays and can create a strikingly different look in certain species, perhaps most notable in oaks and maple. This grain is present in all lumber but its cross-section is so thin that it is nothing more than a very subtle line on the face of a plain sawn board. Picture an antique oak table and you are almost certainly picturing quartersawn white oak; partially for the stability and especially for the medullary grain displays.

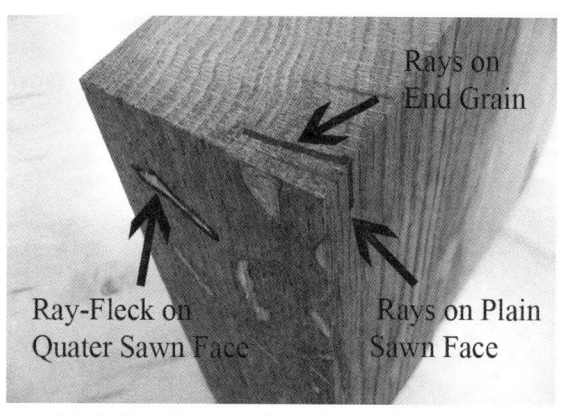

Medullary Rays on three faces of white oak

Still one more distinction within the realm of quartersawn lumber is a further distinction called riff sawn grain. Riff sawn bears the straight lines of all quartersawn, but specifically excludes those boards that contain the figured patterns of the medullary rays. Essentially riff sawn lumber is the "not quite perfect" of quartersawn, but offers the added values of predictable straight grain pattern that is the same on all four sides of the board. This is another character trait that makes riff sawn wood of particular value for table legs or parts where all faces are equally visible, such as the legs of Arts and Crafts furniture.

*Riff-sawn leg with straight grain on all faces.*

## The Urban Sawyer and the Logs they Work From

In a woodlot, logs are "cherry picked", meaning only the best or only selected species are harvested. In an urban setting, log species, grades and yield never dictate which logs are harvested. Even within the unique circumstances of walnut, I cannot point to a case where the log value was a significant factor driving an urban removal. Instead removals are made for other reasons and, log cuts are principally driven by the tree location and removal equipment used by the arborist. Even when working with a goal of reclaiming the log for lumber, location and removal equipment are still the primary considerations. Early discussions between the arborist and the sawyer can be helpful in increasing the yield and value of an urban log. I regularly get calls from arborists who are considering their methods or even their bidding strategy based on what might be possible with the log.

Between removal practices and the generally shorter height of urban tree trunks, high grade logs are not as common. The urban sawyer loves long and straight logs, but they also recognize that many of their logs will be shorter. At the same time, shorter logs may not be a problem for the market they serve. Long lengths are highly desirable for millwork, such as trim in a home or office, but a cabinet or furniture maker is going to cut most boards into small parts anyway. Our mill occasionally gets 14 to 18 foot logs, we've even sawn 20 to 25 foot walnut and cherry logs. But most of our lumber is between 6 and 12 feet long and, with the exception of large live edge pieces, most finished project parts for furniture and cabinetry are well under six feet.

The urban sawyer also tends toward a different approach after the logs have been cut. When sawing urban lumber, log run or mill run sorting (essentially non-sorting) is more common. Why? One reason is that smaller mills with less automation and less volume want to minimize handling. When you don't have a continuous stream of boards in the same species, log after log, day after day it becomes easier to just cut the log to yield the best it can and not be concerned with ripping narrower widths and trimming lengths based on grades. It is far more efficient to just stack full width boards as they come off the mill and, if available, add a few additional logs of similar length and species to the bundle for drying.

Another reason for stacking lumber as it comes off the log—also known as flitch sawing—is that this method keeps wood from a full log or full tree together. Many custom woodworkers prefer working with wood from a single tree because this assures the best possible match in wood colors and character. Log run, mill run or flitch sawing makes more sense for this client base. It also the normal practice for a log being sawn for a specific client who wants something made from their tree.

Perhaps the strongest argument for log run or mill run sawing in the urban lumber marketplace is the defining points of lumber grades themselves. The urban sawyer and the urban woodworker simply ask a different question; what is a defect and what is character? In the global market where supplier, builder and end user may never meet, standards are the only way to define the final product appearance (without actually putting boards in front of the customer). With the potential of face-to-face discussion between source and client, many "defects" are redefined as acceptable character or even as preferred character. Chief among these are knots, unusual grain patterns, heartwood/sapwood and other color variations.

High-character lumber can be located within the commercial market, but these acquisitions are not convenient in that setting. Most high-character lumber is siphoned off the market at the sawmill and sent to pallet makers or other industrial uses, even before being kiln dried. The designer seeking such lumber may have difficulty locating such wood through traditional lumber markets and the retail seller is not particularly excited by this sale since it carries a lower profit margin and any excess inventory will be difficult to sell.

Alternatively, an urban woodworker talking with a specific client on a specific project can literally look at the boards at hand and, with every defect or character trait they encounter, ask "What about this? What about that?" If a particular pattern makes a striking statement, there is a good chance of a matching board nearby in a mill run or flitch sawn pile.

Character lumber is gaining popularity even on larger commercial projects because it is unique and character variations offer something different from the routine of closely graded color-matched, grain matched "perfect" boards. Urban wood is the perfect match for the residential and commercial projects both for their high character and the local stories this wood tells.

Given the logs at hand, the sawyer must be able to reasonably assess each log's potential, then saw the log to maximize that potential. The sawyer will obviously keep grading standard in mind and must have a good sense of what they or their woodworking clients can and cannot use. Even from the best of logs there will be knots and a blend of heartwood and sapwood. There will be wide boards, narrow boards and some that cup and twist no matter how well they are processed. Of course there is also the potential for nails, bolts and other urban unknowns embedded in the wood, all of which needs to be part of the discussion between sawyer and woodworker, and then again between woodworker and client.

**The Sawyer as Artist**

Up to this point, we have only talked about lumber as wood with four corners and three dimension – length, width and thickness. Urban sawyers consider another category of tree to lumber, the art log.

Within most trees there are conventional logs, of whatever grade standard might apply to them, and there are other parts that are normally not considered for their lumber. As an artist or a sawyer who works with artists, there are sections of trees that will never yield lumber that even meets the lowest marketable grade. Grade is irrelevant when the entire section of the tree would be considered a defect. These sections are what I consider art logs.

The Knobby Ash Log... ...Future headboard slabs from that log

Branch unions are primary on the art log list. Where two

or more limbs branch out from the trunk or from each other, the tree must form its strongest wood. In so doing the tree produces its most spectacular grain patterns, particularly in the saddle between the limbs. Within the conventional lumber market, this grain would be labeled irregular at best or firewood at worst. Within the artisan wood markets, this unique grain is called figured or crotch grain, flame or burled – although this last term is not technically correct. Not only is the grain from this particular part of the tree prized by fine woodworkers, but it is especially sought by those who work in live edge designs. The figured grain patterns combine with the unusual shapes of these sections to offer remarkable design potential.

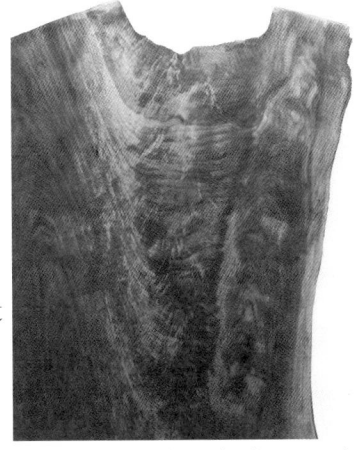

Burls and healed limb scars are another area that does not fit well within the traditional lumber market, but, because of the unique grain patterns they exhibit, these are highly prized for fine woodworking.

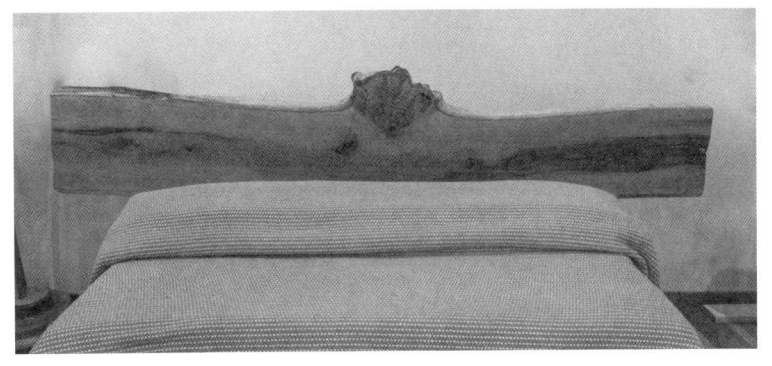

Burled Cherry Headboard

In many ways, burls represent one of the oldest forms of urban lumber utilization, since those familiar with the wood always have their eyes on those trees around them with burls present. When these trees fall, bowl turners and woodworkers within audible range of the chain saw will flock to the site, offering to pick out any parts an arborist or city crew is willing to cut out for them.

Crooks in logs are considered a degrade on commercial logs, since the board yield is lower and the lumber stress during drying is higher. At the same time, the woodworker looking for curved grain for a specific project might be well served by a sawyer willing to cut a curved log. The tables below are just a couple examples of the potential offered by the "defect" of curvature.

Achieving some of the artistic potential within trees may require tree removals being done in manners different than conventional wisdom. An arborist with any commercial logging background would consider the large branch union undesirable and would cut immediately above and below, with this flared section either minimized by trimming or completely tossed to the side. The urban sawyer may instead prefer the branch union be left intact with a few feet of log length below and a foot or two on each branch as well. And, while limb wood is most commonly considered unusable in woodlot trees, the extreme size of limbs in some urban trees makes these parts viable candidates, even recognizing they likely have additional stress within them. That stress may mean additional work, but may also mean additional character.

    Discussions between the sawyer and arborist either before or during removals can guide some of these cuts. Not every cut can be placed where the sawyer would prefer, nor can every part of every tree be utilized for its lumber or artistic potential. Yet, the likelihood of these unique opportunities occurring within an urban setting is far greater than during a woodlot harvest.

# 9
# THE LIVE EDGE PHENOMENON

Live edge is really another term worthy of definition, but where to start.? Tree tips over. Sawmill starts. One cut and you have a log with a flat side; second cut and you have a board with a live edge. Most simply stated, live edge lumber is wood where the edges are not sawn. The "edges" of the lumber are instead left natural, sometimes with bark included, but more often and probably best with bark peeled off. Other terms have been used, but live edge is perhaps the best fit, since the edge of the board is or was the actual living layer of the tree, with every grain ring behind this representing the sequential years prior.

The history of live edge is as old as woodworking itself. From when logs were first hand rived (split) into boards, those boards were live edge. Since the edge of a log is already straight and smooth, there was no need to trim that "finished" edge away. Several years ago I was able to make a trip to Finland and visited several very old sites and museums. One particular memory was a stop at a castle in Turku, Finland, where some original furniture was still preserved. Among those items was a live edge table, really not much more than a flattened log and functionally nothing more than a simple work table, but live edge. Without question, that table, which was several centuries old, is the oldest live edge furniture piece I have seen.

My earliest encounter with live edge furniture design is uncertain in my mind. Somewhere around the age of 14, I was able to take a trip to a sawmill and I came home with a "cookie" or cross-section of a large limb on the side of a log. That slab was planned for a future table from that day, and became my backgammon table in my college dorm room.

Your Author's 1970s adventure in live edge

## Credit To Whom...

Around the same time that I obtained that first live edge slab "cookie," I also saw a magazine photo of a George Nakashima table. I'd like to think I had an original thought and decided to build the table before I saw Nakashima's work, but I honestly cannot say. As I quoted earlier, "There is nothing new under the sun."

Somewhere between the era of the Turku castle and the colonial era, live edge dropped out of the design catalog. I can't imagine decade after decade and century after century of sawmill operators cutting logs and trimming edges without some of them being pulled aside because of their remarkable grain and coloring running from bark to bark. Certainly somewhere out there are some 18th and 19th century live edge furniture pieces. If you have one, send me a photo and the story.

Lacking any examples to the contrary, I am going to give George Nakashima sole credit for bringing live edge to the front door of contemporary furniture design. Yes, there have been period appearances of live edge as we moved to the 20th century, but these were rare during the industrial revolution. So even with the occasional examples from these centuries of silence, I am still going to give George Nakashima sole credit for reviving live edge design.

George Nakashima was born in the state of Washington, but spent almost his entire woodworking career in Pennsylvania, after being released from a World War II internment camp in 1943. From there he gradually built an international reputation for his work in live edge designs, working principally in black walnut. Initially, much of his wood was from his immediate locale, but as his fame grew, so did his network of wood suppliers. In 1983, he obtained his most prized walnut from Long Island, New York and made what he described as the most important design of his career – the Altar for Peace Table installed in St John the Devine church in New York.

Nakashima's plan was for parallel tables in each of the seven continents, but only the original was completed before George Nakashima died in 1991. His daughter, Mira Nakashima, has carried on the family business. She has continued the Altar for Peace tables as well. Subsequent tables from this tree have been constructed and installed in Russia, India, and most recently South Africa.

And most interesting for the purposes of this book, as Nakashima's prized walnut log was being sawn, it was found to contain deeply embedded concrete and a length of pipe. I have not tracked down the history of the tree itself, but it sounds like Nakashima's masterpiece was sawn from urban wood.

## Why this Discussion of Live Edge in this Book?

We substantially discussed how urban wood provides many

unique character traits and allows the artist or craftsman to creatively use certain pieces, but for the most part we have been discussing conventional lumber with four square corners on each board. Even within the smaller shops and overall tree to table marketplace, conventional lumber and more traditional furniture and millwork is the primary production work over the "out there" artistic pieces. And yet, in recent years, live edge has gained enough steam that we need to note how the tree to table movement is a perfect mate to this marketplace.

Simply put, not only was Nakashima's Altar of Peace table from urban wood, but the local wood and urban wood folks that form the tree to table movement are the true experts in the live edge field. Looking into history means we can't claim we are the ones that came up with the idea, but many of us are the people who have produced this lumber and done the designs that have helped grow live edge from Nakashima's roots to the extensive degree you now see.

You see, the same is true throughout history. You can name the big names of the Arts and Crafts era, but neither the Stickley brothers or the Greene brothers had a lock on Arts and Crafts. Instead it was a design movement with many players, all influencing one another. Likewise, Art Nuevo, was not a single individual, but a series of artists with distinct, but linked traits. And the Shaker movement, well ok. In the case of Shaker design we really can or at least should recognize a single society with a specific goal that resulted in a definable and longstanding design; simplicity.

Live edge is reaching that same level. We are now in the midst of a design era, lead in the most part by a single vision, but now being implemented in thousands of unique pieces that are being well designed by hundreds of wood artisans, each with a vision on how to read the log, saw the log, interpret the dried slab and implement impressive designs. By the very nature of assembling these segments of the process, many of these artists are also part of the tree to table movement.

Live edge holds a particularly tight bond for the urban wood scenarios where the project made from the wood is for the owner of the tree. The live edge of the tree represents the layers of growth for that tree in its most recent years. For a homeowner, that means the live edge is the growth during that family's years of ownership. Perhaps I am taking the point a bit too far, but such a tree likely contains carbon once breathed out as carbon dioxide by those family members and their visiting friends. Talk about being connected to your table.

**Not the Stuff for "Conventional Lumber Dealers"**

Live edge is not the typical product of a production sawmill. Sawing logs for live edge lumber takes more planning to maximize the lumber quality. Then, every step of the process requires dealing with the irregular and awkward live edge lumber. They don't have straight square edges, so they don't stack nicely. They are wide and unwieldy, so they don't make uniform width piles. The best live edge log candidates don't even fit on a conventional sawmill. They are just too big, too knobby and downright ugly logs. Nothing that makes live edge slabs desirable is desirable in a high-volume sawmill environment. And, yet, I can't wait for the next live edge call.

Small mills, and particularly those that are also woodworkers, are the folks who are willing to put in the extra effort that it takes to assess, process and slowly dry this wood to obtain its unique offerings. In many cases, these slabs are cut using chain saw mills or larger variations like them, all of which are much slower than the conventional circular mills or band saw mills. This too will change as mill producers develop band saws in the price range of small urban sawyers.

Size itself is another reason why urban wood is a fit for live edge. As mentioned previously, a high percentage of the largest trees are urban trees. We have worked with many trees where a single slice from a tree is wide enough for a dining or conference table. Even more common is a bookmatched table, where two sequential slabs from 18 to 30-inches trees are placed side-by-side to form the full table. These large trees are the ones that both homeowners and their arborists don't want to see turned into firewood or chips.

Drying time is another factor that the urban lumber maker seems more willing to endure. Even the U.S. Forest Products Research Center, the world experts in lumber drying, do not have research on how to dry large, live edge slabs. The answer is simply that this process is too slow for the commercial lumber market.

The best method for drying the largest and thickest slabs is typically a combination of air drying and kiln drying that totals no less than four months and is more typically one to two years.

Then, once dried, the producer must still find clients for the slabs, either as kiln dried slabs, or as finished tables or other products. At our shop it is not unusual to have at least some slabs from any particular log for four years after the log is sawn before the perfect fit for that slab comes along. The commercial lumber industry does not want to warehouse lumber that long while waiting for the right client.

Finally, once the wood is dried and the client is found, you still have more work than many shops might want to handle. We are currently working a 4-foot wide, 3-inch thick and 10-foot long bur oak slab for a tabletop in our shop. Its approximate weight is 450 pounds. The surfaces were cut on our chain saw mill, so it is reasonably flat after drying. However, reasonably flat still meant that we had to take as much as a half inch off each face before we were done. At this width it is way too wide for a planer, so less efficient flatten methods take over. Some shops have a sander big enough, but lugging a 450-pound slab around a sander 50 times is not time efficient. Those that work these big slabs each need to work out a system both for moving the slabs and for flattening and sanding them.

And then there are the cracks and voids and all those other details in the wood that are not compatible with spilled milk in the dining room or signing the big deal on the conference table. I have a 36-inch wide bur oak slab that is perfectly clear on both faces, 3 inches thick and 10 feet long, but this is far from normal. Live edge slabs rarely meet FAS grading standards, but that is kind of the point. These slabs are desired for their character. The knots, splits, voids and other irregularities are all details that the craftsman can work with.

Wood is also an organic material that continues to "move and breath." By that, I specifically point to its moisture content and its moisture content is proportional to the moisture of the air around it. In low humidity the board shrinks, in high humidity it grows. Obviously a good quality finish slows the movement of moisture from wood to air and back, but long, dry winters and hot, humid summers do mean a large board, a board the size of a table, is going to move. A board with funky (beautiful) grain, is going to move more unpredictably. This both needs to be part of the project design and part of the discussion with the client. I just talked with an architect about how we needed to modify his design based on likely wood movement that our mutual client will experience over the life of the desk.

So why do we do it at all? Passion for the work and love of the results. A growing number of custom woodworkers are doing these designs to serve a growing client base that wants them – both residential and commercial. As I write, I have several burled, gnarly huge logs and crotch sections of trees that are in my log yard and ready to saw when weather permits. I know of two more logs that will be coming soon. And then there are five trees, that I can think of, that might be coming out – one is already dead, another is badly damaged, and the others are walnut trees that the owners are just plain sick of cleaning up under. In addition, there is the longer list of perfectly healthy trees that I see regularly, but I'd prefer just keep growing and serving their primary function as long as possible. Call us strange, but those with a passion for live edge cannot wait to see what the next ugly log holds.

**And Some Are Just Faking It**

Good live edge designs are in demand and the extra work and skills needed to produce them means proportionately higher costs. The larger marketplace has seen this, so now there are folks stepping into the field with a corporate view rather than an artistic eye. Live edge is not, by its very nature, mass produced in standardized sizes at a mill that literally grinds the bark and its live edge off the log before sawing the log. But that is no reason to stop the commercial market that keeps getting requests, so they just fake it.

Yes, many products currently being offered are not true live edge pieces. Synthesized live edge pieces are simply boards cut with an irregular edge, then sanded smooth to make it seem more 'natural.' They can accomplish this, in part, but the evidence is in the grain. A true live edge will be absent of grain lines because each year of growth forms a single layer within the wood's grain. If multiple lines of grain show in the edge as they do in the face, then that edge has been sawn, not grown. Yes, even with the best designers working with live edge, there can be areas where an unusual irregularity or log damage may require specific areas to be trimmed and sanded smooth, so small areas of grain may be visible, but if the entire edge shows grain patterns comparable to the face of the slab, it is a sawn edge.

Real live edge on red elm                           Faked sawn edge

A second distinguishing character of many species also makes true live edge stand out – the distinctive colors of heartwood and sapwood within the tree. Heartwood (the older wood in the center of the tree) is typically darker in color, and sapwood (the sap transmitting outer growth rings of the tree) are typically lighter. This color contrast adds significantly to the character of many live edge species. This is especially true for darker woods like walnut and cherry, but is also evident in ash, maple, locust and many more. A synthesized or sawn "live edge" loses this added character trait.

Sapwood/heartwood edges on several species

So, why do we care? Are they not all giving a more natural appearance? Perhaps some of us are just a bit too influenced by the beauty and challenges of working with the real thing so it bugs us when others miss the mark. Part of the reason that it bugs us is simply because the term itself is misused – if it's a free-form edge, call it free form. It is not a live edge if it didn't grow that way.

The more important piece of this is that once you see real live edge designs, you gain a much greater appreciation for how these natural forms simultaneously complicate and enhance the end product design. Each part of each tree is truly unique and reflects the real lines of a real tree that (in the case of urban wood) someone really cared about. This is not a factory assembly line shaping and molding to pre-defined corporate standards.

# 10
# A REAL WORLD EXAMPLE; THE WOOD CYCLE STORY

We've provided a good background on why the tree to table business concept might be possible, but most of us need a real world example. We need an illustration to demonstrate the idea is actually possible. We need a story.

Those stories exist, and as one of the self-declared pioneers in this "nothing new under the sun" marketplace, I will describe the story I know best from having been part of it. Some aspects may be better categorized as history within a market that is now more fully developed, but for some reading this book their local market may still be in its infancy, so our early lessons may be valuable.

This story has multiple components. As an individual business I have operated The Wood Cycle since 2001 and on a less formal basis going back to the mid-1990s. We previously discussed how emerald ash borer and discoveries of other exotic wood pests prompted a more organized response to these pests at multiple levels within both the public and private sectors. One of these organizations that I have been involved with is Wisconsin Urban Wood, currently the largest and broadest functioning urban wood organization. And finally, related to both the above, is a question – would anyone care; other than those directly connected to these issues?

**Your Author and The Wood Cycle of Wisconsin, Inc.** (*www.thewoodcycle.com*)

As a quick background, I am a seventh generation Wisconsin farmboy. I grew up with one grandfather trained as a clockmaker and jeweler, but who became a cabinetmaker. That grandfather jointly owned a sawmill with his brothers, so much of their work began in their woodlots. The scraps from these local hardwoods fell to me and this is where my personal interested and hobby started. My other grandfather was a machinist with woodworking as a hobby. Many other family members were and are artists in paint, ceramic, fabric, wood and metal.

On the broader spectrum of life, I categorize people as either buyers/appreciators or doers. There are those who appreciate creative or well-crafted workmanship, but don't personally have the skills or time, so they tend to be those who purchase this work. Then there are those who do this work more out of a passion, vision or need to create – these are the doers. One is not better than the other; we simply need both personalities to make the arts and crafts industry function. The same buyer/doer roles are probably true in any other industry.

Both sides of my family were fiscally conservative and creative, so it made more sense to make what you needed than purchase what you needed. When our country road was re-built in the 1970s, several cherry, hickory and oak trees were removed, so we loaded them on a trailer and went to a local sawmill to have them converted to lumber.

I share the above paragraph with caution. A trip to the local or urban sawmill is something very few people in modern days get to experience and for a percentage of the general population I can only describe such a trip as addictive.

That experience in my mid-teens taught me things that neither textbook nor You Tube video can even begin to explain. The sights of a log being opened and the incredible grains being revealed for the first time is just part of the picture. Each turn of the log and each pass of the blade translated bumps, arches, limbs and ripples into unique grain patterns that are readily recognized in the lumber yard, but take on a new meaning when translated from subtle details we've all seen on trees. The distinctive smells of each wood species as they are sawn brings its own host of experiences ranging from sweet aromas to pungent odors. I may not have been a normal teen, but I came away from these trips with a greater appreciation for those trees that stood along the road. That, and an eventual career change that I never saw coming.

With that background I went off to engineering school and took an office job that supported my family, but lacked what some would describe as a more robust character. I spent my evenings and weekends feeding this more robust side of life either with a bicycle or in my shop working those very woods we harvested during my teens.

The Roadside Cherry on a Frosty Morning (Upper Right)
Coffee Table from that Cherry Tree

In the Madison area where I settled, as in most mid-size to larger communities, there were a number of one-man custom furniture makers. The trade was in steady decline because the one-man shop is not an easy business. There were and are also a number of larger specialty shops turning out millwork and both commercial and residential cabinetry in a mass production setting. Then there were a few shops that fall in between. These were smaller production shops doing more custom designs, along with conventional hardwood lumber suppliers, smaller millwork shops and combinations of these.

Separate from the lumber dealers and manufacturing side of the industry were a number of farmers with Woodmizer band saw mills. As my woodworking hobby started using up the wood that remained from those earlier sawmill trips, I worked with these farmer-owned mills to produce enough lumber to keep me from needing to buy wood at retail prices. With my engineering background, I also over-designed and built a solar kiln, so the wood I had sawn could be sufficiently dry to build the furniture pieces I produced for myself and my family.

**The Sawmill**

In 1994 I had the opportunity to purchase a used Woodmizer mill and could not pass it up. Spending money purchasing a tool that allowed me to produce lumber was far easier than simply spending money on hardwood lumber. Running my own mill, I justified, would also allow me to decide how a log would be sawn, instead of relying on the judgment of some other sawyer. And with the nearest farmer/sawyer at 82 years old, I justified that someone would eventually need to fill his local niche.

The challenge this mill presented is that I soon realized how enjoyable this added component of woodworking could be. I looked for every sawing opportunity I could, which immediately put me in back yards throughout my area. Every tree came with an interesting story and hearing those stories became part of the sawing enjoyment. It also generated a few woodworking side projects to bring those stories back into the homes from which they came.

I also started encountering tree species that I had never considered sawing before. I was willing to pay to have a good oak, cherry or walnut log sawn by another mill, but butternut, Russian olive, mulberry and even ash were new ground for me. Essentially any log that came along became an experiment that only took time and a sharp blade.

The next sentence will be obvious to those readers that have purchased a portable sawmill. I soon started producing more lumber than I needed to support my woodworking hobby, so the piles grew. Since this all started with the intent of supporting my woodworking hobby, I started doing some side projects to use the wood.

I now better understand how poorly I figured the economics on this, but my first side project was building a butternut kitchen for a friend with butternut logs, in trade for the excess lumber. Then I moved on to cherry bookshelves for another friend, then a maple floor using wood from a front yard tree that was on my bus route as a school kid. Through a series of events that included much prayerful consideration, I soon found myself going to my boss and telling him that I didn't think I'd be there much longer.

When I was considering the transition from desk to woodshop I clearly had no idea what I was getting into. I was an engineer, not a business major. Engineers look for a problem and are convinced they can solve it, so I gave myself plenty of problems to work on. Among them was understanding the value of kitchen cabinetry, compared to the value of butternut logs. Another was that I really knew far less about certain aspects of woodworking than I should, such as finishing. These were all areas I made it through, but areas I probably needed to know better before making such a radical career change.

One complicating decision I made in framing out my business plan is now the basis behind my authoring this book. I decided to distinguish my business by intentionally and exclusively focusing on the hardwoods of Wisconsin. These were the woods I had known all my life and in the years since I purchased the sawmill, I had discovered many more. I was and still am convinced we have some of the best woods in the world growing right in the back yards of southern Wisconsin and hearing the stories behind some of those first trees I cut up helped me recognize that it was not just the Wisconsin hardwoods, but the unique stories that went with these specific trees; these urban trees.

**The Urban Wood Focus**

I am by no means the first to saw an urban log. Others well knew this was a bad idea long before the invention of portable band saw mills. I can't help but imagine that recognizing the potential of urban logs was at least an immediate by-product of Woodmizer's design, if not an inspiration in that design.

Likewise, I am not the first to build any of the projects that have come out of my shop over the years. Kitchen cabinets, fireplace mantles, furniture and wood accessories all go back for generations, if not throughout history. But I was the first, at least in our area, to launch a business focused specifically on the concept of local woods. To that end, I can still claim after more than 50 years as a hobbyist and more than 15 years as a professional, with more than 1,500 projects completed, that I can list less than a dozen projects that didn't involve wood that grows in my own state. Those few exceptions were projects that used reclaimed or salvaged construction lumber, also domestic species just not local.

I'm also among the first, at least in our area, to pull together the complete "wood cycle" under one roof. In reality it was originally two roofs, and then three and now five. Since the start, more than 90 percent of our finished products started either as a tree or a log we had sawn. While many shops will periodically find and have wood sawn and dried for use in their shop, I started my business with an inventory of locally sawn and dried lumber, and I have rarely needed to supplement this inventory with other Wisconsin species that are less common in my specific area.

I was also blessed with a lack of information on what woods are "not worth sawing." Yes, this might be illogical, but for the urban woodworker this is important. The hackberry I mentioned a few chapters back is just one such example. There is absolutely nothing wrong with hackberry, in fact is it currently on my favorites list, but it "officially" has no marketplace. The blessing is that I sawed it anyway, discovered a wonderful wood and built a local marketplace.

Pin oak is another example. I have long known it simply as a member of the red oak family and I learned by experience that even though it is in the most ordinary of hardwood lumber families, it can exhibit a character that is unique from "normal" red oak through its rapid growth. I just learned while doing research for this book that the pin oak I used for a live edge dining table in my home and two others like it in other homes were officially not worth sawing. I still like the table enough to have just picked up another pin oak log of similar size and character.

**Testing an Old World Business Model**

In an era of specialization, I realized I was launching a new business based on a centuries old model that I observed in practice both on the family farm and through my semi-retired grandfather and his brother. I was passionate about wood and was convinced I could combine my woodworking skills with my artistic eye to guide my clients toward a logical best fit for their need. But would this take me beyond the friends and family tier of projects? Rather than focus on a limited product line, I would strive to be the generalist that worked from tree to finished product, making whatever the client next needed, rather than buying a readily available material and building a limited number of mass-produced widgets. It didn't take a business degree to see where that type of business model was headed.

Wood is relational. When you go to an art fair, what is the only artwork that people immediately walk up to and touch? That touch almost defines how the person feels about the work. What I've learned from my customers is they want to "trust the craftsman" that makes that touch possible.

Many of my projects begin with a discussion about what woods are in their home and what local woods are available. Often, if not normally, these are the same woods. Then we discuss the color, grain and character traits of those woods as they relate to their home and their project ideas.

We then move to the shapes that are themes in their homes and how all these details begin fitting together. Because wood is usually a lesser cost compared to the time I will invest in making their project, I first guide my clients to the species based on the best fit for their use. The market value of woods may differ, but I usually price my work the same regardless of which wood they choose, since labor is so much more of a factor than species. Before I've left, we have hopefully developed a relationship that will lead to work in their home, but often there is also a respect for the woods growing around their home. Those are not big-box connections.

Another business feature that was one of those "not normal" aspects of the business model I framed was to offer services ranging from cabinets to furniture, fireplace to flooring, and coasters to columns, along with custom sawmill services and lumber drying. In this era of specialization, offering a broad range of services is a little on the radical side, but I figured Madison could handle a radical idea or two.

    I enjoyed furniture making most, but could see this was not faring well for the one-man shops that were increasingly competing with cheap world market production pricing. At the same time, I did not want to throw in the towel on furniture making before I even opened my doors. After all, I would also be competing against the big-box pricing of large commercial cabinet shops. However, these large commercial shops follow the plan of standardized boxes sized in 3-inch increments lined up side-by-side. So I thought there would probably be opportunities to do some truly customized kitchen remodels.

    Essentially my theory was to find a good client, build the local relationship and offer to produce whatever they next needed in wood. If I've built the trust and familiarity with that client while building a fireplace mantle that ties in aspects of the house and its furnishings, what about their kitchen cabinets, their floor, their furniture or the host of other fine woodworking ideas they might develop? That plan worked. More than 80 percent of my new clients were back within a year for a second project and some have been back more than a dozen times. The side benefit to me was the diversity in products would keep me from feeling like a factory. Every day would offer a new type of work.

    And finally, I considered the scale of business. A good friend and advisor (and regular client) later defined this for me; the difference between self-employment and running a business is employees. As I considered the type of work I wanted to accomplish, I recognized that many of the tasks would take more time, effort and equipment than I could handle as a one-man shop.

    I envisioned a business scale where I could manage the non-woodworking tasks of meeting and designing with clients, writing bids, paying bill and all the paperwork side, while still having time to enjoy woodworking. By having staff I could also divide the overhead costs of the shop, the utilities and the equipment over more work hours, allowing at least some increment of the economy of scale.

Through playing with numbers in ways that only an engineer can appreciate, I concluded that starting with just a couple people and working toward a goal of five to ten staff should allow this all to work. Somehow, as the sawdust settles, and despite the economy of 2008/2009, it seems that these crazy ideas seem to be coming together. After some 15 years, I can sit and write about this right now, then go back to my shop in the morning and feel like I am getting some real work done.

## Efforts to Organize

Almost simultaneous with my business launch, emerald ash borer (EAB) launched its attack. With it came the countermeasures of many local, state and federal agencies as they prepare to fight both this insect and others with which they were concerned. The early stages of the emerald ash borer response were focused on assessing the scale of the issue and the potential impact on both urban economies and woodlands.

In prior chapters we mentioned how one neighborhood association began its efforts by assessing the tree canopy of that neighborhood. This association found that 13 percent of privately owned trees and 24 percent of publicly owned trees within that "typical" neighborhood were ash.

In Madison, and many other communities, plans were formed to define removal strategies and estimate both the workload and economic responds to address EAB, but these plans, at least initially, overlooked the question of lumber utilization. Several years passed and Madison conducted a brief pilot study to saw and market ash in an effort to help raise awareness of the issue. More time passed and an ordinance was developed to create a pathway through which municipal logs could flow to sawyers, but each of these steps was a slow road, encouraged by key individuals and then key organizations.

That same neighborhood organization that conducted the tree inventory decided to move from assessment to action through subsequent grants that allowed them to pull together a coalition of interested parties, ranging from arborists to sawyers to custom and artisan woodworkers. As an established urban wood business, The Wood Cycle was among the invited members of that effort. Initial discussions explored efforts to coordinate with city and county plans, but without EAB findings in the area, the further details on how those plans might play out remained vague. Members from the Milwaukee area shared how they had managed to build the connection between the city and a mill in that area, but they likewise recognize this was only a first step.

Both the sawyers and the woodworking business members of this group emphasized that without market development, the entire utilization strategy was irrelevant. Massive stockpiles of ash could be sawn and dried, but someone needed to use it. The Wood Cycle and others could promote our individual businesses, but a more uniform message and more consistent brand recognition would be needed if we wanted to increase the marketplace enough to use the ash and other urban woods that were already available. Efforts largely shifted toward marketplace development among the private sector members, while dialog continued with municipal and county representatives in hopes that the long-term strategy was not limited to just privately owned trees and the work of independent arborists.

Combined efforts of the Madison and Milwaukee-based

members were beginning to show promise. In Milwaukee the focus was on larger commercial interests that could manage and move the higher volumes of lumber already resulting from EAB removals. In Madison the focus was more on the artisan and small custom shop. Both scales of the urban lumber economy were, and are, of interest.

But the question still remained as to whether the broader public cared. Finding urban logs did not seem to be a problem, even with limited wood being sourced from municipalities.

Sawing lumber was not a challenge, several mills were operating in both the Madison and Milwaukee areas and none were operating at maximum capacity. Drying kiln capacities were not abundant yet, but all the members recognized that as the market developed, the private sector would rapidly meet any kiln needs that market would demand. But, before the private sector would scale up capabilities, the question of whether there were buyers that cared needed to be answered. A test of the market was needed.

In the Milwaukee market that test was partially met on the commercial scale by a high-profile project that intentionally used urban ash from the community. The Clock Shadow building not only included urban ash removed because of emerald ash borer, but ash that exhibited the full range of character we expect from urban ash. Members could not only tell stories, but could now point to pictures and say look, see what is possible.

## The ReStore Experiment

In Madison, another market test followed. With the recent success by Recycle Ann Arbor and their expansion to the Genesee County Habitat for Humanity ReStore in Michigan, Madison tested these waters. The Wood Cycle was well established at this point and through our expanding network of homeowners and arborists we were consistently offered more urban logs than we needed for our work. We decided to test the market through a Habitat for Humanity ReStore location in Madison.

For those not familiar with the ReStore concept, Habitat for Humanity is a long-standing charitable organization that works through churches and civic organizations to build homes for families that could not otherwise afford a home. As a fund raising component for those home construction projects, Habitat for Humanity formed ReStore as a chain of retail stores that sell locally donated building supplies including both used materials and excess inventories supplied by homeowners, builders and remodelers. The retail locations are staffed partly by volunteers and revenue from the stores support local Habitat for Humanity building efforts. ReStore seemed the perfect test market for urban wood for several reasons:

- ReStore had an established client base that was already oriented toward reclaimed or repurposed products.
- ReStore covered the building supply product line including reclaimed construction lumber, so their clients were already oriented toward construction-related projects and would be in that mindset as they were shopping.
- Being an established charitable organization, customers recognized their money would be going toward a good cause.
- While urban lumber, as we define it within this book, was not exactly a recycled product, it fit within the realm of reclaimed, repurposed and upcycled products.

And if the test market proved successful, additional long term benefits would include:

- Added Habitat for Humanity revenue.
- Private owner log suppliers could feel good about donating

logs knowing they would find a good use.
- Municipalities could justify donating logs knowing the donation would benefit a local, reputable charitable cause.
- The same strategy could be employed in additional ReStore locations throughout the country.
- The urban wood branding concept could continue growing through a network of homeowners, hobbyists and small custom or artisan woodworkers.

    Under our plan, The Wood Cycle pulled unused kiln dried urban lumber from our inventory. Each board was labeled to identify the species, zip code in which it grew and the price for each piece. Pricing was intended to reflect local retail costs for respective species, while also considering the generally higher production cost for urban wood. For the less-common species the pricing reflected what seemed a fair market value for the unique offering. For the pricing system to be sustainable, we believed the overall pricing would need to reflect the actual production cost for urban lumber, including the normal retail mark-up that a for-profit business would require. ReStore agreed to cover our actual processing costs and the difference between these costs and the fair retail value of the lumber would be their income stream. Essentially, this ReStore model could best be considered a wholesale/retail agreement between an urban wood sawmill/kiln and a non-profit retailer.

    The initial test consisted of a lot of about 150 board feet of lumber in various species and of varying quality (representative log run material). A small display explained that the wood was sawn from urban trees in the Madison area and the logo below that is now used by Wisconsin Urban Wood was developed to market the 'new' brand. The response was immediate and very positive. Within three weeks the lumber was sold. A second shipment of 300 board feet also sold out in three weeks and sales have continued to grow from there. Urban wood is now offered at both Madison ReStore locations and other Wisconsin Urban Wood members are supplying several additional locations throughout the state.

Comments from ReStore customers focus on a few primary points.

- Local – Many buyers report they first look to see what they can find from their zip code, then expand to whatever else they might need for their specific project.
- Width and Character – Buyers appreciate finding wide lumber, even if it has knots. As we have found in our own shop, sometimes there is an added sense of adventure in determining how to most efficiently lay out parts around knots or even incorporating those knots in just the right locations.
- Variety – The final prevailing comment of ReStore customers is the variety of local wood species available. Both our shop and ReStore staff are regularly asked by clients when the next shipment will arrive. Interestingly, while "bad boards" at a typical lumber yard are picked through and left, this is not the case with urban lumber at the Restore location. From monitoring the ReStore inventory, we've learned that literally every urban wood offering finds a home, all without needing to offer them at a discounted sale price.

**Formation and Growth of Wisconsin Urban Wood**

Perhaps inspired to some extent by the ReStore experiment and probably more by a factor of timing, the neighborhood study that expanded to a Madison/Milwaukee network was now ready to formalize its existence. After discussions on whether each area should form its own group or whether we should claim our efforts as the basis of a broader foundation, we launched

# A REAL WORLD EXAMPLE; THE WOOD CYCLE STORY | 157

*www.wisconsinurbanwood.org* as a planned statewide organization.

With the practical limits of geography, we acknowledged unique working clusters in the Madison and Milwaukee areas. These clusters represent, two larger metropolitan areas separated by less than 80 miles. The distance is far enough that arborists and sawmills are unlikely to bridge the gap, but close enough that some custom woodworkers could span the bridge and lumber could be shared between the clusters when local supply and demand justifies the trip.

In 2014, Wisconsin Urban Wood was open for membership. That initial membership year included 13 firms and individuals, consisting of arborists, sawmill and kiln operators, custom woodworkers and other interested parties. Within a year another cluster formed in the Eau Claire, Wisconsin region, another 180 miles distant. By early 2016 membership had grown to over 30 businesses and individuals.

While much of the growth was existing businesses with an established interest in the field, many of these members also represent either entirely new businesses that formed with an intentional urban wood platform. Consider that just a few short years ago, I doubt anyone could name more than a half dozen businesses nationally that were involved in urban wood production or utilization, and now *wisconsinurbanwood.org* offers a list of several times that in just a single state.

Wisconsin Urban Wood is still early in its existence and is still working out answers to questions as they appear, but it is already having several impacts:

- Better networking between arborists and sawyers through defining what logs are most desirable and better connecting

scheduled removals with those that can use the logs. At least within arborist members, more logs are reaching sawmills than previously occurred.
- Better networking between sawmills and lumber users. Individually mills can saw any log that comes, but historically you could only invest that time if you had a place to go with the wood. Between the growing markets and the knowledge of who is using what or who might have what, there is no reason to not saw any worthy log that shows up.
- Better marketing. By having a greater network and a brand that can be shared between a number of networked members, the organization is better equipped to sponsor public events or make presentations before broader audiences. Consider that just a few years ago Wisconsin only had a few disconnected sawmills that stocked urban lumber, but may not have even tracked or marketed that lumber as anything distinct from their normal operations. As of this date, I can identify 10 retail locations within Wisconsin selling urban wood, all under a common branding strategy, while still representing their individual corporate identities.

While the emerald ash borer is continuing to spread across the state, ash is only a small component of the overall view within Wisconsin Urban Wood. Yes, ash may represent between 10 and 20 percent of the trees in some southern Wisconsin communities, but that means 80 to 90 percent of the trees are other species, many of which are also of interest by woodworkers and many of which come down every year, each for their own set of reasons. This broad basis will sustain the tree to table movement well after the ravages of EAB are past.

# 11
# TREE TO TABLE ECONOMICS

Using economics as a chapter title is a good way of losing my audience, but it is worth the risk. In this movement we are re-introducing old-world economics much akin to the practices we are seeing within the farm to table movement of the food industry. Two main points come to mind when we discuss tree to table economics, the first is how this all fits together to form an economically viable system and the second is the finances behind the equation. We will attempt to address both, but without being too detailed on dollar values that will certainly vary from one city or region to the next. We will speak first to the systems that make this all work.

As described in the prior chapter, The Wood Cycle and many other independent businesses have formed over the years with urban wood as a part, if not a primary component, of their business. Certainly some of these businesses have found success and others have come and gone, yet I would suggest that few urban wood businesses would describe themselves as thriving without some degree of networking with like-minded businesses. Woodworking is a financially challenging profession on its own. Working urban wood just further complicates the matter. And yet it is possible. I was never the only island out there and certainly am not any more.

Perhaps the greatest impact those of us involved in Wisconsin Urban Wood are observing is how inter-connected each of our unique and formerly independent businesses are becoming. In recent years we can also lay credit to an improving overall economy, but the networking efforts within Wisconsin Urban

Wood are certainly furthering each of our individual businesses. Within this network, members are routinely communicating on what logs are coming out where, who has what lumber available to fulfill orders and who needs what lumber to complete their project.

We still function as independent businesses and are competing against one another, but we are increasingly comfortable in guiding people to other members who are a better fit for the question at hand. In sharing a united brand identity, we are also better positioning ourselves as the buy-local concept continues to blossom.

Having said this, most of the Wisconsin Urban Wood network member businesses are less than five years old, or less than five years into the urban wood component of their business. This window is a commonly viewed "make it or break it" business timeline. With this in mind, how will each of our individual businesses fair in the coming years?

Individually, we are certainly like any other new ventures where some will thrive and others will not. Each business has to learn their strengths and weaknesses and then focus their business toward their strengths and shore up those weaknesses that remain essential to their overall operation. They need to establish a market share and please their client base within that market. In a new or expanding market the earliest entries have a better chance of survival, but only until new businesses fill the local demand or out-perform the early entries.

In recent years nearly every woodworking trade publication has written at least one article featuring a local business that has captured attention for working with urban wood. Our practices are not an oddity any longer, it is a nationwide trend. A quick internet search will identify a number of custom woodworkers focused on the use of urban hardwood logs. Depending upon your search parameters, you are also likely to find just as many, if not more, custom woodworkers or retail outlets offering salvaged industrial lumber. We previously noted that salvaged construction lumber is not the focus of this book, but we simultaneously recognize many shops that use urban hardwoods also encounter projects where this salvaged lumber is an appropriate or even best fit.

The most successful urban wood businesses will need to build connections with other like-minded businesses within their communities. The tree to table movement is dependent upon a number of players we previously introduced, all fulfilling unique functions within the overall movement. If one player's needs are being met by the others within the system, then their desire to fulfill their function is encouraged by those other players. Just like the Bible verse that says all parts of the body are needed for the church to function well and if any member suffers they all suffer; so it goes with any other networked organization.

What seems most likely is that the tree to table movement will continue growing. There are too many positive aspects to the concept, particularly in a culture that is grasping ever more firmly onto the concepts of sustainability and local economies. The only likely failing would be for the movement to go the path of too many other industries within the global economy, by short-cutting their processes and reducing product quality. If we fail, we likely have ourselves to blame.

**Value of Urban Logs**

The quick answer to what an urban log is worth is little or nothing.

To keep this all in perspective, consider that a woodlot-grown hardwood tree will yield three to four logs of better quality with very little steel in them, all with a market value of perhaps $100 to $200. Higher value species and larger size trees may go higher, but many trees are even less. In addition to generally higher quality logs, there are many logs at one location and all the junk wood and limbs can be left where they fall.

These woodlot harvests also employ heavy equipment that can move multiple logs with ease, some without a single human hand touching the tree or its wood until the individual boards are sorted based on their quality. A fully mechanized logging crew may move several hundred logs to a landing in a single day. Commercial log values recognize these volume-based efficiencies all the way from the stump to the lumber rack.

Now look at this from an arborist's perspective. The arborist is dealing with a shorter tree that may have only one or two logs with a true market value of $25 to $100. If they are managing a full-day removal project requiring a three to five-person crew, how much time can they afford to invest in those couple logs? Typically, the biggest cost component in an arborist's calculations is getting the tree on the ground. Then, once the tree is down, it is already later in the day and the priorities shift to the most efficient way to pick up and clean up the jobsite before leaving for the day. With equipment scaled to fit into a backyard, the larger the log, the more difficult it is to remove in a salable length.

Final disposal of the removed material comes at the end of the day when the crew leader has mentally if not physically moved on to tomorrow's work and disposal is a final step on the way back to the shop. While the arborist might be bothered by disposal of a nice log, it is easy to see why the added steps and coordination may not be at the top of their priority list. Log values are a small detail in their calculations. Again, thanks to those arborists who care enough about what they see to not just take the simpler path.

Finally, look at the urban log from the sawyer's perspective. A sawyer can get ready access to woodlot logs that are straighter with fewer defects and with next to nothing for nails or other hardware. They can produce more lumber of better market grade value when sawing, and they will have less down time from unseen hardware. By locating closer to larger and more remote timber stands they both save on log transportation time and probably find lower cost labor and pay less for their business site. Why would anyone within the lumber industry mess with urban logs? For the most part, the commercial industry simply doesn't. Even I have asked myself this question many times, and yet I still do it.

With all this in mind, we can look at four principal factors that influence log value, whether that log be urban or woodlot sourced: species, size, quality and location.

- Species relates to desirable traits of the finished product. Walnut and cherry are well recognized woods with a strong market demand, so these logs tend to have higher value. Regardless of the other factors, some species do not have a well-established marketplace and have an automatically lower value, since specific buyers are harder to find.
- Size, or for that matter the number of logs available at a single time and place greatly impact value, since the time commitment to pick up one log verse five, or a small log versus a large log may be much the same. Costs are typically not that much different to pick up a full semi load of logs.
- Log quality relates to what can be expected from the log. Size can play a big role on log quality. Quality, however, may not follow traditional log grading standards, since the urban sawyer tends to look at a broader client base than most lumber yards. A traditional straight and clean-looking log is obviously desired for traditional lumber whether grown in a woodlot or backyard. Although, if the log is being considered for live edge lumber,

bumps and knobs might not be a down-grade. A larger branch union, for example, might make the urban sawyer think figured coffee table slabs or kitchen island tops, while the commercial logger is more prone to see waste material. Essentially all this falls to the artistic eye of the sawyer, based on past experiences with similar shapes.

- Location, location, location. Ideally, one log is located next to the next, next to the next—a woodlot setting. In a woodlot, the mess can be left behind and a day's work is measured by the semi-loads produced. At the opposite end of the location spectrum is a single log in a tight back yard with limited access. That log typically has a cost, not a value. A good log at the front curb or along the driveway is likely cost neutral; probably about the same value as the cost to come pick it up. A pile of several good logs in the arborist's yard that can be picked up when time permits almost certainly has some value. And, finally, a log delivered to the mill almost always has some value. If there is a pile of those logs with good size and high quality and in the same species, value is evident in most any species. That, again, is usually the woodlot scenario.

Any one of these points can be a make or break an urban wood proposal. Even in those circumstances where I am discussing value that a tree may have, I must point out that this is all secondary to the primary service of the tree and the decision to keep or remove a tree must usually be made on the assumption of no value. If the tree is rotted or found to be loaded with nails during removal, the value immediately drops to zero and the log must still be removed.

## The Municipal Log

All these above concepts and valuations also apply to the municipal log and yet there are also differences. Principal among those differences is the economy of scale issue. The municipality also makes individual tree-by-tree removal decisions and generally focuses on the least healthy trees or removals related to construction projects. Many of their trees are comparable in size and quality to the backyard trees, but the municipality has more of them and those trees are less likely to contain nails and bolts. Yes, there are individual arborists who may out-scale a municipality, but that is the less common scenario. Some of these larger arborists actually exist because their clients include municipal governments. Municipalities and larger arborist are also more likely to build connections with places for their log production volume, whether that is firewood production, pallet making sawmills or more conventional mills. In those cases, the urban sawyer is just one of a few possible markets.

Log value is a more complex issue for a municipality as well. It is easy to say a log has no value and just give it away. In fact, one common approach is to simply have a yard where wood and chips are dropped and anyone can enter to get either chips or firewood. This is perhaps the most common small-town scenario and the one many would prefer maintaining as long as possible. Yet that system has also been known to break down when a higher-value tree comes down and a line forms all claiming they were there first, or they should have first dibs. One municipal employee shared that their log yard shut down after they found residents arguing over a log, both with chain saws running.

A variety of alternative approaches have developed and many more will certainly follow.

- Agreement between municipalities and individual wood processors have been effective when there is only one interested processor within the municipality or where one or more processors are willing to provide some in-kind service

back to the community. I can point to examples including lumber for the high school woodshop, finished products from the logs for city facilities, or lumber given to nonprofits or other worthwhile community causes or efforts. I am sure there are more informal arrangements as well.
- Contract agreements between municipalities and individual wood processors can be effective, particularly when those agreements lessen the municipality's costs, such as providing a disposal alternative, especially by accepting all wood products; logs, limbs and chips.
- Contracts between municipalities and an insured urban wood network is a new entry on the playing field. Under this option a municipality simply limits yard access to privately insured members of an also insured urban wood network. The agreement provides better control over the yard while also assuring those with access are experienced and insured for what they do.
- Log auctions are another approach, where better logs or even firewood lots are periodically offered for sale.

**Value of Urban Lumber**

      This can be an equally difficult question. In the eyes of some wood users, lumber is just a commodity with its price solely dependent upon local supply and demand. Under this viewpoint, cherry is cherry is cherry and if good quality cherry is worth $6 per board foot, then urban cherry is also $6 per board foot. A board foot, again, is the volume equivalent of a one-square foot at one-inch thick and is the standard measure for essentially all hardwood sales.

      Others, your author included, see urban wood as fitting a different standard. Urban wood is just starting to work its way into "green" or sustainable certification standards, but most observers very quickly understand that this wood is probably as environmentally responsible as any wood could be. These clients are purchasing the concept, rather than a simple commodity. These are the clients who will support the urban wood movement even if it sometimes has higher production costs. On the scale of their project and after weighing the local, environmental and social perspectives, a growing client base is seeing urban wood as a greater value.

Having said that, a higher actual production cost per board foot is almost certain. The sawyer or the arborists and others who supply that sawyer have gone to a greater effort to procure generally shorter and poorer graded logs using less automated equipment and operations. They dry the wood using smaller kilns that require more manual monitoring and less automated loading and unloading methods. All these operations take place in or near generally larger urban areas, where both wages and the cost of living tends to be higher than most commercial mills and kilns. Were it not for savings on the multiplied shipping costs and the associated warehousing etc., of the larger woodworking marketplace, urban wood probably could not compete.

But then there are also the stories that go with urban wood. Woods that have more value because of their history than because of their species. Often these stories alone tip the balance in favor of urban wood, which of course goes back to the point of purchasing a concept rather than a simple commodity.

Finally, urban wood declares its character. Because the commercial sector cannot or chooses to not cater to the broad range of requests from custom woodshops, wood artisans and wood hobbyists, some urban wood simply fills a unique and growing market demand. Not that urban wood is by any means restricted to the hobby user or the artisan, but the ability to serve a local craft industry with these unique cuts provides a secondary market for a less common inventory; an inventory that happens to be a larger part of urban mills simply because of the logs they receive. By careful evaluation of the logs and assessing log potential based on local market demand, the urban sawyer can successfully serve both the artisan and the larger commercial client

Because of these factors, price per board foot is not a simple number, but more likely a range. The same is true in commercially graded lumber. How much does cherry cost? That depends on what you are really asking:

- What thickness, length and widths are you seeking?
- Do you want FAS, No.1 Common or lesser grades?
- Are you talking about all heartwood or what ratio of heartwood to sapwood on each face?
- Do you want curly grain, plain sawn grain or any other specific patterns?
- Are you asking for a single board or 1,000 board feet?

Answer all the questions and any lumber dealer can nail down the price, at least for that week. But if the answer to that final question is too small of a quantity, then it may not be worthy of that dealer's efforts to even track that lumber down. That's fair. How long would you spend talking to various suppliers and organizing shipments for a one-time order on which your employer can only anticipate a mark-up of a few dollars?

In reality, a typical lumber yard does not ask you all those questions. Instead, the lumber yard answers all the questions for you, based on what sells best for them. You simply have one to perhaps three or four piles of cherry from which to select, each pile with a set price.

The urban wood market is comparable, but the inventory

options instead include whatever the local landscape has offered over the prior year. I currently have five thicknesses of cherry, with varying lumber grades within each thickness, depending upon how each board is trimmed. Some of the wood has lots of sapwood, some does not. Some is curly, most is not. Lengths from 4 feet to 16 feet are common and a few are up to 25 feet. Widths from 4 inches to more than 20 inches are common with a couple live edge slabs up to 50 inches.

Why so many choices? That just happens to be what our landscape has supplied in the last couple years. If we specifically sorted my inventory, I would likely find every grade in every thickness, but to do so would be a poor use of my time. Instead, I ask my client to tell me what they need and I will see if I have boards that will get them there.

So how do we price urban lumber? Three common scenarios emerge.

**Traditional Grading Rules**: In this scenario, grade decisions are likely made at the point of sale. Boards may or may not be pre-priced, but the retailer simply does their visual grade evaluation and prices the board consistent with NHLA grading standards and charges accordingly, at whatever board foot rate is locally appropriate. If the retailer uses this approach, they are more likely to trim defects to improve the grade, so the boards are likely to be smaller than when they came off the mill.

**Log Run or Mill Run Pricing**: This is probably the most common approach for larger quantity lumber sales from an urban mill. The sawyer will cut the best they can from the logs they get, but they do not further sort the lumber beyond removal of the poorest quality boards. Log run versus mill run is merely a question of what degree of poorest boards is included. Using this approach, the sawyer likely leaves boards as they come off the mill with very minimal trimming on widths or lengths. The whole pile moves through their system without further grading or sorting, except that the poorest of boards are extracted. On log run a few more poor boards are pulled than on mill run. As noted previously, however, the overall quality of log run or mill run lumber depends upon the quality of logs that the lumber is sawn from. The buyer can accept it based on their knowledge and trust of the source mill, or they can look at representative boards from any specific batch to get a sense of whether that pile was cut from high grade logs with a good yield, or lower grade logs with lower yielding lumber.

**Useable Board Feet**: This is essentially a combination of the above methods, considering grade, character and size, all under the subjective eye of "how might this board be used?" Essentially lumber sold under this approach is graded by a more subjective standard that considers their specific market and uses within that market, typically focusing on smaller commercial shops, artisans and hobbyists. Lumber is likely sawn based on a log run approach above, with the sawyer deciding how to get the best yield from the log. Once sawn and dried, individual boards are assessed based on the useable area of each board. The seller considers both the size and character of the board to determine possible uses and how much of the board might be used under those circumstances. Some defects under NLHA standards may result in the seller considering the board smaller than its actual side, other defects might simply be considered character. Pricing then reflects those considerations and the local market value. A couple examples might best illustrate this point.

**Example 1:** A board that is 8 feet long and 12 inches wide at one-inch thickness. Technically the board contains 8 board feet. This particular board has several knots along one edge. If all the defects were cut out, the board would yield a perfect board that is

9 inches wide. Under log run or "useable board feet" approaches, the board is sold with defects included. On a log run approach the whole pile is just sold at a price that reflects the mixed quantity. On an individual board sale, a useable board feet price assumes only ¾ of the board is useable. The price is sold based on six useable board feet multiplied by that seller's board foot price.

**Example 2:** This board is 12 feet long and 8 inches wide, also at one-inch thick, which also contains a total of 8 board feet. The board has several cracks at one end and a large knot in the center. This board cannot be trimmed to yield any better grade and the same log run approach applies as in Example 1. Under "useable board feet" the seller concludes one foot at the end of the board is not useable and six inches out of the center will not be useable. So, 18 inches of length at 8 inches of width is one square foot of surface area, or one board foot that is not useable. There are several very small knots elsewhere on the board that are considered part of the character and are not discounted as defects. The seller concludes this board has seven useable board feet and prices the board based on that.

**Example 3:** This is a live edge board that is 18 inches wide, 4 feet long and two-inches thick. The board has several knots and the live edges have a lot of unique shapes caused by the grain swirling around the knots. This board does not exist under traditional grading and probably would not be batched in a log run sale. The board is unlikely to yield any sizable cuttings without knots, but with its width, live edges and substantial grain character, it would make a nice bench or coffee table. In this case, what traditionally would be considered defects are dismissed and the entire slab is considered fully useable. In fact, given the unique nature and demand for something like this, it might (and probably should) be considered worthy of a premium price.

## The Special Case of Walnut; Log and Lumber Values

Walnut trees are attractive, but they are also lousy yard trees for other reasons. A walnut with its hard green husk is the size of a tennis ball and several times its weight. For several weeks to a month each year, these nuts arrive without warning from up to 80 feet off the ground. Over this period each year, a single tree will deliver bushels of nuts. Once they hit the ground, the husk softens to a black pulpy mess that stains roofs, decks and driveways; still leaving the hard-shelled golf ball sized nut as a potential lawn mower projectile.

Additionally, juglone, a secretion of the walnut tree family that is especially strong in black walnut, can make gardening or even growing grass beneath a walnut tree difficult. Yet in communities such as Madison, the biggest walnut trees seem to hide in urban areas. Why? The answer goes back to economics.

For a large woodlot, walnut economics are simple; is it veneer grade or just a saw log. Veneer logs in walnut regularly sell for two to five times saw log prices and for the right log in the right market, veneer values can go even higher. Hence on the commercial level where every party looks for the best price on their slice of the pie, why would one not sell all they can toward the veneer market? Would a commercial sawyer willingly saw a perfect veneer log into lumber? Gladly, and the lumber will sell immediately and for a premium price. But those logs will never reach a sawmill, because the log buyer can make better money selling them to a veneer mill. The sawmill cannot top a veneer buyer's price unless they establish a long-term premium market for large clear boards. In a volatile lumber market, it is not worth that risk. So with log quality and size dictating end use and value, a woodlot harvest is planned down to the specific trees to be removed and the specific trees to be left, either to maximize the landowner's profit, maximize the buyer's profit or meet a specific dollar value based on the landowner's family economics.

For urban walnut, the fiscal criteria differ. Here the economics relate more to the cost of removal and cleanup than the value of the log. The primary decision is not economic benefit, but the value of eliminating the nuisances of falling nuts, stains and lack of ground cover versus the cost of removal and loss of an otherwise beautiful shade tree. Compared to those bigger questions, the value of the actual walnut log is a secondary.

Urban logs, with their hardware issues are a poor choice for veneer. Because veneer logs values can be significant, they are individually tracked and traceable back to the original seller. As that log is shipped half way around the globe, its value becomes increasingly higher. So when one or more of these logs is found with steel and cannot be used, that veneer mill can trace it back to the original seller. Understandably, a logger known for selling logs with steel to the veneer market will not be in that veneer market for long.

All this plays together to the advantage of the urban sawyer and their clients as well. All the hassles of managing a single tree that were previously mentioned still hold true for walnut, and yet the experienced arborist still recognizes the unique nature of walnut. These arborists are more likely to contact an urban sawyer because of the potential value of a walnut tree than for any other log. They are also more willing to take the extra efforts on a removal for these logs than any others.

In turn, once the sawyer gets an urban walnut, they may well find better lumber than their counterpart commercial sawyers will see. Yes, they risk hitting nails, screws, bolts and concrete, but we've well established that the urban sawyer is accustomed to these added burdens, even for lesser wood. Once processed, I would argue that urban wood producers are likely to have some of the biggest and best walnut lumber on the market, and their regular clients are the first to know.

High-figure walnut is a secondary component of this picture. These are the big logs that would not be of interest to a veneer buyer anyway because they have too much unpredictable character. The big and bumpy walnuts, are also heavily biased toward urban settings and are a particularly good fit as we consider live edge walnut. For live edge character, veneer is not our goal, we want extreme figure, knots and whatever an urban log can throw at us (except hardware of course).

So after all this, what is an urban walnut log worth? The quick answer is "generally far less than the rumors."

It seems that everyone with a walnut tree has heard walnuts are valuable and on a relative basis they are. At the same time, so is the cost of removal and, logically, the larger the tree the higher the removal cost.

My first response to anyone asking the question is not to give them a number, but, instead, I start with an explanation that the value of an urban walnut rarely exceeds its removal cost. This can save a lot of time if the only reason for the call is the idea of potential profit. I'll be honest that I have worked on a couple cases where the log value exceeded the removal cost, but this is only in very exceptional cases. Even in these unusual cases the economics were not at a level where they drove the decision. One was a clear safety concern, and a couple others were probably more of an economic wash rather than a profit and were removed because of building foundation concerns.

Once economic gains are set aside, the removal discussion more appropriately circles back to how well they like the tree and the shade it provides, versus how annoying or dangerously they view the nuts, stains and bare ground beneath the tree. If they still plan for removal based on those factors, then I am willing to venture an estimate on the potential log value. I will also direct them toward arborists who understand the urban sawyer's perspective and know how to maximize the log value from these trees. And of course, I will also raise the question of having something made from their tree. That, after all, is the best use of a tree once removal is planned.

**Value of Finished Product Craftsmanship**

Whether talking about the prized backyard walnut or any other urban tree, the next economic question falls to the value of a product crafted from urban wood. Obviously this is where the term craftsmanship is a key component.

Craftsmanship is a cross between skilled trade workmanship and artistry. Think about what other skilled trades you purchase, whether that be your auto mechanic, plumber, electrician or hair stylist and look at the hourly rate for those services. Some of these trades require extensive equipment, but can you point to any with an investment greater than a woodworker? Even a smaller full-service custom woodworking shop will have no less than $50,000 invested in their equipment and many tip the scale at well over $100,000. That does not include facility purchase or rental, taxes, utilities, vehicle(s) and consumable supplies. All this gets reflected in hourly rates.

Now consider the life of the product. You will likely spend far more on your car than on your bedroom or dining set, and, yet, which is more likely to hold its value in 10 years, and which is more likely to still be in service after four generations of use? The true woodworking craftsman is really an antique maker.

Finally, add in the stories behind that wood. The cherry table photo at the start of the prior chapter, for example, was from a tree that grew on my family's farm. That tree started as a seedling while my great grandfather owned the land and grew until it came down because of a road reconstruction project when I was young. The table will likely pass from my parent's home to one of their grandchildren, and from there it is just a question of stylistic preference as to who would get it next. The table will certainly be strong enough for generations of use, even if it needs to be sanded and refinished multiple times over these generations. What value is appropriate for such a family heirloom?

Stories even have value within the commercial sector. On the multi-million dollar renovation of the University of Wisconsin's Memorial Union, what items received attention at the opening reception? Yes, several major contractors were thanked as were significant donors and stories were shared about several key components of the projects. But one of those key items was a single oak tree that needed to come down and became a part of the interior woodwork. Total cost was perhaps a couple tenths of one percent of the total renovation and yet that story was among the lead stories on the opening night.

Doing the right thing is just another aspect to the value of the tree to table movement. As LEED building design criteria and Forest Stewardship Council certification standards begin to wrestle with the "small" story of urban wood, we remain hopeful that appropriate recognition also lands here. Doing the right thing can have direct economic value in the right circumstances, whether it be improved aesthetics from the materials chosen or customer or employee loyalty that comes with the right corporate attitudes.

Like craftsmanship, handmade is a term worthy of definition. And yet finding agreement on what either term precisely means would be impossible and probably unfair to some. Neither directly implies a one-of-a-kind status, but certainly both imply limited production scales. Neither requires only hand tooling, but both imply human skill over robotic automation.

All these terms add value in a world marketplace where mass production of short-lived and poorly crafted work dominates. Unfortunately, we cannot directly assign a value on any of this, since those values are as unique as the products, their producers and their clients.

## Parting Financial Thoughts

Having considered all of this, the best answer that can be supplied to the question of economics of the tree to table movement is perhaps a bit over-simplified by saying you likely get what you pay for.

- An urban log has value only if its woodlot counterpart has value, but in a single log scenario it takes most of that value to get it to the sawmill.
- Urban lumber cannot be produced as cheaply as the big mills, but with its unique properties and its service to a boutique wood market, this wood seems to be providing sufficient market value to justify the production costs.
- The craftsmen using urban wood to produce custom work or small production runs cannot mimic big-box pricing, but neither are they stopping at big box quality. Their work might be best compared to higher-end furniture or accessory stores, but with a more honest rendition of the term "custom" and with the added benefit of a story; a local story, if not even a family story.

# 12
# SUSTAINABILITY BY ANY OTHER NAME

In more ways than not, the overall sustainability movement is merely a return to former practices. New devices, safer equipment, greater productivity, but more sameness than difference – simply with a generational shift.

Instead of living and surviving in a harsh environment, most of us live in a sheltered city and are culturally distanced from our "real" environment. If we are cold or hot, we adjust the thermostat. Snow means "plan extra travel time" instead of "we might not see our neighbors for the next couple days."

Likewise, a trek out in the wilderness has changed from leave enough of a trail so that you can find your way back to use your GPS and leave only footprints, or how many bars will I get for a cell phone signal. And, while we like to complain about weather forecasting, it is on the whole still accurate enough to plan almost any event. Consider that just a few generations ago, checking the forecast meant following such sayings as "red sky in morning sailor heed warning, red sky at night sailor delight," or simply recognizing the ache in your bones as warning of a pending storm.

As a child on the farm I learned to love the land in a way that few outside the farm environment can understand. The land was our lifeblood. If it rained, you had a crop. If not, you lived with what the earth gave. On a cold day you worked outside, on a warm day you worked outside, on a wet day you worked outside. If the weather didn't permit the specific project you had in mind, you adjusted to other work that always needed doing. Boredom was not an option. Lazy days were not an option (except on Sunday).

You also learned to respect the environment in ways few today understand. I can still recall the day my mom was coming home from town and got stuck in the snow within a half mile of home. This was some 30 years before the first cell phones, so all we knew at home was that she was due home soon. Our road was only five miles out of town, but, there were only two homes and it wasn't a shortcut to anywhere. It was also known locally for heavy snow drifting. By mid-winter it was a single lane wide with 10 to 12 foot snow banks on each side.

Sitting there stuck in the drift, my mom knew there would be no traffic the rest of that day and it would be at least a day and may two before the road would be plowed. While staying with the car is the conventional wisdom, she considered how long she might be stranded and knew how close she was to home. She decided to walk that last half mile in white-out conditions. My dad, by the grace of God and knowing she was overdue, continued his outside chores, but kept an eye toward the road. He eventually saw her wandering near the road, delirious from the cold and not realizing she was within 50 yards of the house. Although this was only about 40 years ago, it was a different time than most in the sustainability community know.

So, not withstanding my current career choice, I am a bit of an outsider to the more conventional sustainability movement. I spent 20 years in a setting with a staff of scientists and engineers dealing with both real and perceived environmental threats and fears of the unknown – some threats that might be real and others with no bearing in truth. At this job, I knew the processes, the protest methods, the compromises and the flat out ridiculous positions that some individuals or groups would take just to win their point, whether scientifically justified or not. And these came from both sides of the aisle.

All this posturing was part of why I made the change to wood. At this same time as I was moving out of this political hotbed, a number of environmental groups, big lumber companies and timber owners were duking it out on what eventually became the Forest Stewardship Council certification process. In Wisconsin just under half the forest lands, public and private, already qualify for the FSC standards that eventually came out. The question is: are these lands in better hands than before? Maybe. A better reality is that for these standards to be adopted so broadly and so rapidly, simply shows that much of this land was already being well managed. That's why Wisconsin's timber stands continue to log net gains in timber density.

I decided to stay out of all that. At one time, early in my business I actually got a printout of the full documentation process to show the wood I got from just one timber harvest met the FSC standards. The paper trail (or the print version of the electronic trail) ran from floor to ceiling, and that was just up to the point where I picked up the logs to saw them and produce flooring. How much time, travel and type were spent to document that those 15 trees were "green?" I figured if I just stuck to local woods, and as I further transitioned to almost entirely urban woods, I could not only avoid the "big-boy" environmental game over wood, I could beat it.

And that we have.

For starters, urban trees only come down when they must, not because they are ripe for harvest. Once harvested, they rarely travel far. In my case "exotic wood" means it came from the next county over, not the next country over. Many of us in the urban wood system can tell you specifically where the tree stood, and if we don't already know, within a couple phone calls we could probably tell you who owned the tree, the address at which it stood, why it came down and who did the removal.

All that said, my point is that this chapter may not follow all the "traditional rules" on defining sustainability. I'm not the activist taking a stand, nor am I the timber baron trying to rape and pillage a pristine environment. I have clients who sit in both political and ecological camps. But like I stated, those debates can all stay in the job I left, it's not where I want to spend my time or my efforts in this book.

Instead, consider this book being written not so much by myself, but by those who most inspired my work, starting with the conservative Dutch families of Oostburg, Wisconsin and the family farmers of Berlin and Omro, Wisconsin. You likely don't know these places – they are small Midwestern towns with rural economies.

I grew up with the understanding that you use your God-given gifts and the resources around you to make what you need and to support your family. In the process, you don't destroy those resources, because that is what you would later be passing down to your children and to their children, as had happened on our farm for six prior generations. As it turns out, what I was taught as "responsibility" is in perfect alignment with what we now call sustainability.

My point is that regardless of which background brings you to this page, the end result can be much the same. As the author, I get to define sustainability of the tree to table economy on my terms, yet I believe this definition will land us in a place upon which we can all agree, without anyone feeling they need to compromise anything. At the same time, I hope this chapter will challenge your thoughts on at least some items that are often being viewed or touted as sustainable.

I proposed that sustainability within the wood product industry needs to consider at least these three aspects, which we will then consider in greater depth:

1. **Responsible resource management**—the short term or "green" measurement
2. **Durable goods that are durable**—the long-term look
3. **Economically viable**—the lasting business model view

**Responsible Resource Management**

Sustainability itself is most often intended to mean good for the planet. Good for the planet, however, is often connected with an advertiser's or speech writer's agenda, and that agenda becomes more important than cold, honest truth. The agenda might be to "support my cause", or even more specifically, "buy my product." Unfortunately, the variety of twisted agendas linked to the term sustainable mean we need to look behind the curtain every time we hear the term.

The case of urban wood is probably one of the cleanest pictures on this stage, despite our sawdust. The removal of almost any tree in almost any urban setting is upsetting to someone. The debate is not about the wood – it is about the tree. And given the economics of urban wood, tree removals are rarely if ever linked to an economic gain regarding the wood. Most removals are controversial because people prefer the trees over the new condo project, or the trees over the new pavement or the utility upgrade.

None of these issues relate to urban wood, they all relate to the value of a tree versus the value of the project or the value of public safety. They are questions related to tree vs. no tree, and those are not agendas into which the tree to table movement plays. We do not come into play until someone has decided the tree will fall, but the tree debate assures no trees are removed without cause.

Once the decision is made and the tree is on the ground, everyone concurs that finding the highest and best use for the wood is a good thing. The questions are merely what that highest use might be, and who might want to help that happen. The pathways and purposes for which logs make their way to urban lumber processors vary, but I've yet to hear of a case where anyone was upset about a log being up-cycled from landfilling, chipping or even firewood.

    Efficiency in process is the next question. For comparison we need first consider the conventional woodworking process discussed early in this book, with all its multiple players and all their trucks and boats. Urban wood rarely follows this multi-step scenario. For finished products I produce, well over 90 percent of the wood never travels more than 50 miles from tree to mill to kiln to shop to final customer. For lumber we sell, most of my clients are within that same radius and the few clients I have at greater distances are those who are specifically seeking out urban wood over conventional lumber and can't fill their specific needs any closer to home.

    We certainly win the sustainable question based on transportation, but what about other processing perspectives?

- Are our saws and kilns more efficient? Not necessarily. Having said this, my observation is that urban mills measure dollars spent carefully, so increased drying time often trumps purchased energy, which sometimes means the wood can be at least partially air dried, or solar kiln dried. In those scenarios, we certainly would win. Also I would venture that a greater percentage of the wood actually sees its highest and best uses, since urban sawyers tend to work with lower grade logs than the commercial mills ever see.
- Are our shop operations more efficient? Again, probably not, at least not at the surface level. Generally, the small custom shops focused on urban wood are less automated, which means less manufactured and purchased equipment. Equipment itself has

a huge up-front energy and resource impact that is not often measured in sustainability assessments. In the long run, the labor savings of automation may eventually offset that up front impact. So it all depends upon how you measure your carbon footprint, and over what timeframe. One could also question whether the full footprint includes the manpower aspect. The traditional sustainability models tend to bias toward the idea of manpower over machine power, but pancakes and pizza are also consumed carbon turned to greenhouse gases.

- What about our products? This we win hands down. Our small custom shops focus on solid lumber that is locally sourced and most often locally sold. Solid lumber certainly sequesters carbon and requires far less energy and glue and mechanical processing than processed particle board furniture, regardless of where it is made or how efficient the machinery might be.

    Using the responsible resource management component of our definition, I need to contrast urban wood with bamboo. I've chosen in my business to stick with local woods, so given that bamboo is not technically a wood at all, I could simply dismiss the issue entirely. Yet we must address bamboo because it is so heavily marketed as the "green" or, "environmentally responsible" material of the wood industry, based solely on the fact that it grows so rapidly. Rather than me spending countless pages sharing my views and research on bamboo, I suggest you instead do an internet search on how bamboo flooring is made. Be sure to search out the harder to find sites that are buried among those sites that are trying to sell you their product. Their agenda is obvious and so is their bias.

    Bamboo is simply fiber; fiber that needs to be glued up to make a product. We like to think it grows by itself, but in our current economy it is plantation grown, fertilized and sprayed with chemicals just like any other crop. For those of us in the U.S., we also need to recognize it is fiber shipped here from the other side of the planet, while we sit in a country where timber is growing at nearly twice the current rate of harvest. The finished product retains some bamboo-like character, but in all truth, grass laid straight and flat does not have much character. If you want clean straight lines, consider riff sawn oak or for that matter, riff or quartersawn ash, both of which are native to the U.S., and both of which will outlast your bamboo.

Let me move on by simply asking how sustainable it sounds to ship a heavily manufactured product half way around the world when we have an alternative that requires far less processing and is literally growing in our own backyards? I must, of course also admit my bias, but I think my argument is both convincing and justified.

**Durable Goods that are Durable**

When I was young, "Made in Japan" was a somewhat derogatory term to suggest cheaply made. As Japan's economy got rolling, the "cheaply made" sticker changed to "Made in Taiwan," then "Made in China," now "Made in…" As each country's respective economy and production capabilities get rolling, cheaper labor moves next door. Some would say it helps them, some would say it exploits them, neither is the point of this book. We simply need to admit we live in a global economy, so we are part of both the good and the bad.

The point again, is that we have always had a "cheaply made" label. In the 1700s, America was likely that label for Europe. In any era, however, that label really falsely labels the country of production and instead needs to be "owned" by the person who writes the specifications for what is an acceptable product. The work leaving my shop is defined by my shop standards. Not every piece is perfect, but I decide what is acceptable and what is not, all based on what I think my client is expecting. The same is true for every shop. If Japan's work was less than what an American customer expected, that is only because the 1950s American distributor that wrote and enforced the specifications decided a lesser expectation was acceptable.

    The same holds true today. As already mentioned in the opening chapter on the history of woodworking, the trend has been well established on our overall willingness to compromise quality and durability for price. Not that we are always willing to do so, but as a culture we have certainly bowed in that direction and accepted those cuts often enough that disposable furniture has become the norm instead of the exception.

    I think of a local furniture store ad I've been hearing where the seller is pointing out that to sell their clients a furniture piece that will only last a couple years is not a good value. They would rather sell their clients "a piece that will last ten years." Ten years? Wow. Anyone know a woodworker who is excited about pouring their heart and soul into a custom piece that their client will be tossing in ten years?

    If we define craftsmanship as the intersection of technical excellence and artistry, I feel the tree to table movement is currently well endowed. Not all our artistry will stand the test of time as styles change, but we certainly don't approach our work with the intent of replacing it in ten years or less. When I build a dresser I use design principals and joinery methods that have stood the test of time. Specific style preferences may change, but the construction methods anticipate that it will be passed to the next generation, and hopefully to several more beyond.

    Having said this, the overall movement is still in its early years, where the involved individuals are first-tier owners with a high level of pride in their craft, and that pride telegraphs into their workmanship. As this tier of ownerships starts getting bought out or transferred to the next generation, that pride of workmanship might slip into production mode in some cases and in other cases it may well grow to a new level of craftsmanship. But first, these businesses must pass the next test of sustainability.

**Sustainable Businesses Last**

This part can't be missed, yet is often overlooked. Sustainable is often just looked at from an environmental standpoint, but if those businesses within these environmentally sustainable fields cannot sustain their businesses, then the entire system breaks down. We could debate the merits of subsidies to promote or support sustainable models, but eventually any business model should be self-sustaining.

In large part this question is still yet to be determined. Some 80 percent of new businesses fail within the first five years and most tree to table players are still less than five years into the field, or at least less than five years into the urban wood aspect of their business.

In essence, the first question is whether the business model itself is viable. Certainly some businesses can live in this marketplace. There are a number of businesses, mine included, that are more than ten-years old and have formed with urban wood as a substantial if not majority focus of their businesses. Whether these firms are exceptions to the rule or merely older examples of what is to come will be answered over the next decade.

Likewise, the second question is survival of the urban wood networks that are forming to support the businesses striving to make this work. As long as the urban wood businesses remain truly small businesses, these businesses will survive best with the support of a network of like-minded individuals that can share log and lumber supplies as needed to fill client orders.

In the end, it is the client orders that will determine survival of the tree to table movement, hence defining sustainability for the tree to table movement. Market development continues to be the dominant concern and interest of those businesses in this emerging industry. A good number of firms have well established that the interest is present, but awareness of the urban wood industry is still immature and the volume of interested clients is yet to be determined.

The real sustainability question may well come after the assumed success of the movement. Whenever capitalism encounters pronounced success, those who see a new way to make a quick buck move in. Let's just look at the term "sustainable" itself as an example. What company, regardless of product or true "environmental correctness" is not trying to grab a part of the green market or the sustainable market? Must I mention bamboo again? Energy efficiency? Durability? No, the real question is what can my marketing department say about my product that makes it look or sound consistent with the buzzword of the day.

If the tree to table movement builds sufficient brand recognition it could become a target for brand piracy. I am hopeful that our methods and workmanship will build brand recognition worthy of a premium price for our high quality wares.

The added complexities of producing urban wood and building well-crafted products locally, all under a fair American wage system is not the pathway of the global market, but it is a good pathway. If the tree to table "brand" does become a valued market, one can simply imagine that someone somewhere will short-circuit the process by not truly sourcing urban wood or by departing from fine craftsmanship to poor quality workmanship.

## Carbon Footprint

And finally who can write a book that mentions

sustainability without at least once using the term carbon footprint? I've probably created enough controversy by this chapter already, but I have to play this one out just a little. As a woodworker, after all, I am in the carbon business.

Over the years I have completed several sustainability/green related assessments, all with good intents for programs that did make sense to me. The problem is that they often missed the point of our work. Compare my business with another business in an identical facility down the road that uses commercial lumber that started as a tree somewhere, almost anywhere else on the planet and they will likely rank just as high. If it is bamboo or wood from a FSC certified source on the opposite side of the planet, there is a good chance their paper trail will outscore mine. Why? Urban wood does not yet register as an "equal" in the carbon economy, when by all the measures I can imagine, it substantially out-performs the alternatives.

Scoring systems that focus on assessing a carbon footprint are fine, but don't bank on them. Urban wood leaves a better carbon footprint than any paperwork trail can.

# 13
# NEXT STEPS

Without question, the tree to table movement is launched. Many small businesses are well engaged throughout the country and many more are either forming or gaining an appreciation for the urban wood options around them. Yet, in many regards those working urban wood are treading new ground within a woodworking industry that has changed substantially over the past century.

Much of what makes our businesses unique is our departure from many of the business models. In the tree to table movement, there is much less specialization, mass production and multi-state marketing campaigns. Imports are completely absent from this scene and if there is anything in the export realm, I would be virtually certain it would be finished products.

However, departure from these world economy business concepts should not mean departure from all things business. The tree to table movement still follows other good business practices, and will need to do so in order to be sustainable in the long term. We need to develop a consistent message so that we are not so unique as to be irrelevant. We need to expand our market presence and, as a poster child of sustainability, we certainly should receive recognition for those aspects of our business model.

## Growth in Organized Networks

Wisconsin Urban Wood is the largest and most broadly functioning tree to table network currently functioning.

Yes, I admit a bias on this point, but consider:

- The network includes both municipalities and individual land owners who serve as the source for urban logs.
- The network includes private arborists and consults with their municipal counterparts.
- The network includes both small and medium-sized sawmills and kiln operators along with their associated wholesale and retail brokers and storefronts. Sales are occurring board-by-board and in commercial quantities of log run graded material.
- The network includes custom woodworkers serving both residential and commercial client bases with a wide array of products and services. And the network has developed a sustaining customer base for its products and that customer base shows promise of continued growth.
- Finally, Wisconsin Urban Wood is involved in moving the industry forward on a national level by working to achieve its appropriate recognition within the realm of architects, designers and sustainable certification bodies.

But Wisconsin Urban Wood is mostly about Wisconsin. Most states, regions or large municipalities do not yet have organized representation of their industry. Most businesses are still islands in their respective urban jungles. Some would prefer this; some even like having the pie to themselves and might resist the idea of competition or shared branding. That is understandable when you have put in the efforts needed to launch this industry. But there is considerable room for this industry to grow and uncounted others are certainly ready and waiting to jump on board, if they only knew how to connect.

Not every arborist, urban sawyer and woodworker using urban wood need necessarily join such an organization, but there are many lessons to be learned from doing so and the industry will grow as a result of these shared efforts. We are not unlike any other trade group that recognizes the power of coordinated efforts.

At the same time, to the extent such organizations do grow, they also need to become self-sustaining. Wisconsin Urban Wood was launched through the organizational efforts of a committed few and was partially supported by state urban forestry grants. Grants still provide a portion of the operating funds. However, as emerald ash borer moves further through the state and nation, these grants will wither like the trees. Being both a hardwood lumber state and having been one of the earliest groups to organize have both played to Wisconsin's advantage and is part of the reason we can be effective on efforts that will have both state and national impacts. But even here, if Wisconsin Urban Wood cannot make the transition from grant support to fully member funded, the model is not sustainable.

Toward that end, Wisconsin Urban Wood already charges membership fees in addition to our many volunteer services and we continue to explore other funding options. Specific membership rates will continue to require reviews as we move forward.

As part of this effort and because of its growing leadership role in this networked approach to urban wood utilization, we are also donating a portion of the revenues from this book toward Wisconsin Urban Wood and plan to do likewise toward parallel organizations as they form. *www.past9publishing.com* contains a listing by state of those organizations that we are aware of and also identifies those with a 501 C (3) tax exempt status for those who wish to directly support these organizations.

## Market Development

From its pre-name meetings through today, public education and market development have been key components of Wisconsin Urban Wood. The same holds true for member businesses that are simultaneously trying to firmly establish and grow their businesses. This is true not only within Wisconsin and its network members, but it is true nationally.

From our experience, awareness of the option of using urban wood remains the primary business impediment, second only to an assumption that true custom work is unaffordable. In our discussions at trade shows, I am regularly surprised at how often I hear people commenting they were not aware anyone did this anymore or that they assumed the costs would be unaffordable. Either I am underpriced or our costs simply are not out of line with good quality work from any other source, whether local or from across the world. The truth probably lies somewhere between these two.

Market development will likely follow multiple paths. Wisconsin Urban Wood seeks out events and exhibits, in addition to speaking and media opportunities that are likely to reach our target audiences. Let's face it; this book is one such opportunity. Individually, our businesses each seek out those tools most effective for our individual niches within the greater niche of urban wood. Shared brand development and utilization of common branding efforts by members of Wisconsin Urban Wood further builds recognition of the broader market. Inversely, identification with that broader market can help pull customers into a company-specific booth or ad.

And finally, we must always remember that the tree to table movement carries with it a great story—reclaiming our resources, public and private sectors working together, unique product offering, all with a local angle. Provided this new industry maintains high integrity and high craftsman values, all these, along with traditional advertising and trade shows can only build the market and help eliminate the "I wish I would have known about this when my tree came down" stories.

## Standards Development and "Green" Recognition

Perhaps more on the commercial project side, Wisconsin Urban Wood members have also been working to develop specifications and standards that describe urban wood in terms used by architects, designers and commercial project specifiers. Standards are the lifeblood of the commercial project industry.

While we have previously emphasized how urban wood departs from the existing standards, we can simultaneously embrace the development of standards that recognize the broad range of character we can expect from our diverse lumber source. These standards combined with example photos we are currently developing will allow our future clients to grasp the potential of urban wood and gain a sense of what might be possible for their finished projects.

One specific example of an urban wood architectural specification standard can be found as you scroll down the home page of *www.wisconsinurbanwood.org*. Using this specification as a starting point, the architect or designer can further declare what components of that lumber are to be included or excluded or specifically managed in the overall design. Traditional defects can instead become features that attract attention to the fact that this builder used locally sourced urban wood.

U.S. Green Building Council, LEED and FSC recognition are also among the next steps. When I started drafting this book, these were all well-established, sustainability minded programs that I viewed more as distant goals for the tree to table movement. My current hope is that the following text will instead be one of the first areas of this book to become dated material.

The U.S. Green Building Council is the premier North American organization for sustainable building practices. While the organization provides guidance for all levels of construction, the mostly commercial LEED (Leadership in Energy and Environmental Design) certification program is internationally recognized as the model for green building. LEED certification promotes sustainable construction by using a point system to rank construction sustainability both in the construction process and in post-construction energy efficiency. Points are issued for a wide array of environmental and conservation related construction considerations.

Until now, urban wood has been noticeably absent from the list of materials and practices recognized by the LEED program. This isn't surprising given that the urban wood industry has literally been emerging from the woodwork in just the last few years. LEED points can be earned for using recycled or locally sourced materials with local defined as less than 500 miles. Given that, urban wood certainly qualifies for these locally source LEED points, but there is so much more to the story. Urban wood is typically source from wood that would otherwise be destined for waste disposal (or firewood at best), then it is typically processed and installed, all within 50 miles of its origin. And all this is while offsetting consumption of "native" or traditional wood resources. I would suggest that any program aimed at sustainability on a global level should specifically consider products that are extremely local and distinctly repurposed from the waste stream, all while sequestering high levels of minimally processed carbon. Urban wood is hopefully on this path within the LEED system.

Similar to the LEED issue is Forest Stewardship Council or FSC certification. Instead of looking at sustainability from a building products perspective, FSC certification looks at sustainability of the wood growing and harvesting practices, to assure those practices are sustainable. As such, LEED logically offers bonus points for using FSC-certified lumber.

But urban wood is likewise noticeably absent from the FSC world. As a starting point, FSC begins with certifying the woodlot source and the management practices of that source area. FSC then develops a chain of custody system to track this wood to its end use. In the timeframe of FSC's development urban wood was not on its radar. Even if the urban wood marketplace had existed as it does today, its relative size was, is and will likely always be very small. So, under current systems, wood grown in a woodlot across the planet receives greater environmental recognition than wood grown within a few miles of where that wood is being used, and using trees that are only removed when they must be, rather than being removed when they can be.

Currently within the FSC system, a possible scenario is recognition of municipalities with well managed forests, which they generally are. Blanket acceptance of this concept that urban trees are well managed and only "harvested" when there is a need would be the ideal scenario, but city-by-city acceptance of this truth is at least a first step. Again, we will learn more on this aspect of recognition as the next few years unfold.

**Source Documentation**

Recalling that I came out of a bureaucratic desk job environment to form my business, I find this section very hard to write, and yet true success deems it will become necessary to protect our efforts. If all we strive for within the tree to table movement is effective and the market does in fact grow, and urban lumber is in fact recognized as a premium product, then fraudulent opportunists will follow. That is an unfortunate way of the world.

Like with the chain of custody process under FSC certification or documentation of authenticity of an urban source may become necessary. This would again fall within the realm of brand protection, likely at the organizational levels of groups like Wisconsin Urban Wood.

The documentation would not likely be needed from a standpoint of verifying sustainable management and harvesting, since we have already established that urban trees are not removed for profit, but only when their removal is necessitated by other considerations. Instead, the purpose of documentation would simply be to verify that the brand labeled "urban" wood was from an urban source. Without such brand protection, any log from any source or any finished product from any lumber source could be claimed as "urban" for the premium value urban sawyers and craftsmen hope to establish. The need for a uniform certification system may also come sooner than I expect.

# 14
# HOW TO CONNECT

Here is where the book switches from passive to active.

As I've previously emphasized, success of the tree to table movement is a question of sustainability. In this book, I've defined sustainability not only from an ecological standpoint but I've also emphasized the importance of product durability and business viability in our definition. Taking this one step further, business viability is a combination of a good business model, quality craftsmanship and market demand.

Market demand comes down to people like you. Without market demand a perfectly good business fails. With moderate market demand good businesses succeed, and with great market demand existing businesses thrive and new businesses form. People who care about this topic, and more specifically those who care enough to have both picked up and read this book, are among those who define sustainability for the tree to table industry.

After nearly 20 years of working with urban wood at the core of my business model and seeing how many similar businesses have formed since then, I know that the concept of using urban wood is viable. As both a viable and sustainable industry, the next step is to connect individuals with those who are already moving this industry forward.

Our website, *www.past9publishing.com* contains a state-by-state listing of the individual businesses and organizations that I have learned about over the years. This listing includes both businesses that mill and kiln dry urban hardwoods and those that subsequently work that wood into finished products. Many do both.

These are all folks who care enough about this industry to have contributed toward seeing this book published. Those listed in Wisconsin are Wisconsin Urban Wood members, and as such are peer reviewed into our organization, so I'm comfortable attesting to their workmanship skills and business ethics. I have met many of those listed in other states as well, but just by distance I know less about their daily operations and business practices. On the whole, the final decision as to who is the best fit for your project needs to be the result of your own interview process, not mine. I do, however, want you to leave this book with the resources in hand to give you a starting point on who is working urban wood in your area.

Our website listing contains many of the leaders within the urban wood industry, but not all of them. Without question, if you do an internet search in your locale, you will find more businesses working with urban wood, and five years hence you will likely find even more.

Currently "urban wood," for example, will identify many of the names our website identifies, yet it will also identify many others that exclusively or primarily work with reclaimed or salvage lumber. There is nothing wrong with this work, in fact most of us in the tree to table economy also work with reclaimed lumber. But reclaimed or recycled lumber is a very different aesthetic and a very different material. Reclaimed lumber is most typically softwoods like pine, and Douglas fir, where the character is mostly the distressing caused by nails, paint, holes and dents on the surface.

In the case of urban hardwood trees that have been sawn into lumber, the character is all about the grain, the coloring and the character of the woods themselves as they grew in an urban environment in your lifetime. If you are specifically looking for the tree to table movement I have described in this book, you need to dig down to those businesses and organizations that speak directly about urban trees removed for various purposes as defined back at the start of this book.

Secondly, focus first on your geographic area. If you have a specific craftsman or a specific wood in mind, you may need to search farther from home, but the whole focus of the tree to table movement is to start with the local economy, then go beyond those local walls as needed. Ideally, you, or your wood, will never need to travel across national borders or the entire planet again.

**How to Select Your Urban Wood Arborists**

Everyone with trees has the opportunity to connect with the tree to table movement any time their tree needs service. A good arborist has a first interest in helping you preserve your tree (see Chapter 6). Some tree services are more focused on expanding their scope of service by suggesting removal when a trim will be sufficient, simply because the bigger job is good for them. You want to find an arborist who doesn't automatically assume removal is the only option. If removal is needed, whether because of health or location, then seek an arborist who is connected with an urban lumber network, if such a group exists in your area. If not, at least include questions about options for urban wood utilization within your interview process. In Wisconsin, many of the members of Wisconsin Urban Wood organization are arborists who want to see trees they remove going to higher purposes than mulch or firewood.

**How to Select Your Urban Lumber Producers**

A professional urban lumber business is likely to make the urban wood aspect of their business known. Quite simply, we are proud of the unique work we do, we have gone through the extra hassles involved in producing this wood and we know the unique character of this product. Why would we not want you to know?

But an urban lumber producer may or may not deal exclusively with urban wood. If there is a mix to the business, they should be ready to distinguish which is which. Additionally, the urban lumber producer should be willing and able to tell the stories behind the wood they offer. It should be such a natural part of their vocabulary that once you bring up the history of the wood, you should have to quiet them down – the passion for their product should just leak out. Some will know the specific trees, others might just know their local sources. Either is better than the alternative lumberyards.

In our case, we pick up more than half the logs we mill, so we often know the specific address and the reason for removal. We also track historically significant trees because we know our clients care. For our other urban wood, we simply identify it by the zip code from where the tree came, or the city or county of origin if that is all the detail we have. Ask your supplier what unique lumber they currently have and you should be able to walk away with both a board and a story.

Perhaps most importantly, remember that most urban trees are removed for a reason, with health of the tree primary on the list. As one urban lumber producer among a growing many, my primary concern is that this entire industry play by the same standards as the big commercial hardwoods sector. We want the wood properly dried and heat sterilized to kill all life stages of all insect pests. Specific recommendations on this will vary, but lumber that moves in commerce as kiln dried has reached about 8 percent moisture content and has been heat treated to no less than 140 degrees Fahrenheit for no less than 3 hours per inch of lumber thickness. The key is that the core of every board everywhere in the kiln exceeds 130 degrees Fahrenheit for at least an hour.

Air drying and solar drying are both great and can

accomplish most if not all the drying aspect, so we also employ these options. But without a specific heat treatment step, neither solar or air drying alone will achieve the insect sterilization. Remember, emerald ash borer, just one example of a major infestation we now have in the U.S., got started because someone moved lumber that was not kiln sterilized. We do not want to further such problems. Be certain to ask specifics about how your lumber supplier dries their urban lumber.

**How to Select Your Urban Wood Craftsman**

I again note that the craftsmen listed on *www.past9publishing.com* are not a fully pre-qualified list with regard to price, quality or reputation, but this is a great starting point. You need to meet your craftsmen and find out what they are all about. Certainly start with what you've learned here, but check them out directly or through their other local clients. Generally, you are using the same criteria you would use for any other skilled trade, whether plumber, auto mechanic or computer technician, but hopefully your
craftsman can add an artistic eye that your plumber may not offer. So consider all the questions you would ask when looking to hire any other professional service:

• How established is the business? Are they full time vs. part time (is their livelihood dependent upon your satisfaction)?
• Can you view their workmanship in person – either via a showroom or at local galleries?
• Can you talk with or do you already know past clients?
• Do you sense they have a passion for their work? Or do you feel you are just talking to a salesman instead of a craftsman?

Those questions should help you understand who your

craftsman is, but that is only the first step if your real purpose is connecting to urban woods. Find out specifically what they can tell you about the woods they might be working with for your project ideas – is urban wood a natural part of their vocabulary? Do they know where the wood comes from or just how locally it is sourced? Can they share any interesting stories connected with the trees they currently have to work from?

Within the WUW organization in which I am a founding member, new members are qualified by existing members, based on what they know about the member candidate from a skills and business ethics standpoint – our membership becomes meaningless if membership in the organization becomes meaningless. Do I know every member? Not personally, we are a statewide organization. What I do know is that other members I trust know them, so I have that level of comfort in making a more local recommendation.

At the same time, I recognize that some of my partners are also competitors, and that is fine. We currently have several WUW members in my local market. As we meet there is some jovial jousting among friendly competitors. Likely at times, we will be bidding against each other for some clients, but many other times we are working to build an industry in which we both win.

What about pricing of the urban wood craftsmen? I will go back to another biblical quote on this point: "The workman is worthy of his wages." Your urban wood craftsman is competing with a world market against cheap foreign labor, but they have the same regional cost of living as you do. They also compete with the world economics of a mass-production lumber industry, but work with wood that is tougher to harvest, mill and work with. The urban wood craftsman cannot be giving their work away; unless your craftsman is an impassioned retiree who is just using their hobby to justify the next tool purchase.

At the same time, the urban wood craftsman does not have as many middle-man mouths to feed, so their prices may not be as "out of reach" as you might think. Workmanship of the local craftsman will so far exceed the durability of the big-box imports that it is an apples/oranges comparison – a bookshelf with shelf life of a few years verses a bookshelf with a life beyond your own.

A fair comparison on quality and pricing might start by going to the best furniture stores in town to see what is being charged. Look very closely at the details of construction, the wood character, the fit and finish. Then go to your local urban wood craftsman and compare on a basis of craftsmanship, character and pricing. It will be quickly apparent if you have found the right craftsman.

Design, personality and passion of the craftsman will combine with the character of the selected woods and the precision of the work when the fit is right. If in doubt, go back to the furniture store and take a second look just to remind yourself of the alternative, both in quality and commitment. If prices are even close to comparable, where would you rather see your money spent – supporting your local economy, or supporting the global marketplace? Often you will find the local craftsman can offer options and added value that make the choice obvious. If not, perhaps you just have not found the right urban wood shop for you or for your specific tastes. Chances are, they are out there, also looking for you.

**Or……..Be the Craftsman**

Perhaps your reading of this book is simply a transition process to the next level of involvement. Perhaps, instead of looking to purchase a furniture piece, you are scoping out the tree to table movement as a potential career path. Hopefully this book is also an inspiration for some to join in this more direct manner. If so, welcome.

We would have stopped at the last sub-heading if we didn't think there was not yet another chapter, if not a whole book to be written. Why would we invite more competition if we didn't also realize that this competition sharpens us all? But before quitting the day job, a few words of advice:

**You will not get rich quick.** Tree to table is not a get rich quick scheme. It is not even a get rich slowly scheme. "Get rich" and "fine woodworking" are not in the same vocabulary. We have covered the levels of competition you face from the world economy. We live in a world that sees and hears furniture store ads daily that ingrain in us that we can purchase a full dining or bedroom set for a mere $500 to $1,500. That is not a pricing structure sustainable within the urban wood marketplace. It is not sustainable in the world economy either if considering all the aspects of sustainability defined in this book. Still, both the big-box store and the hobbyist down the road are very real market competitors that need to be considered and will always be there.

**"I could do that" is not your friend.** Oh, the bane of every artist, and yet a phrase we have all at least thought, if not spoken. We have all seen art that we just don't get and maybe even believe that we could do ourselves. But even in those cases, "could do" and "did" are different. The eye for design is one aspect, a waiting client is a second, and the actual skill to pull it all together is a more distant third.

In the specific case of urban wood furniture production, using the unique shapes and character of urban wood is a blend of engineering and artistry. Simply put, some people are good at this, some not so. Balance, proportion, historical designs and a long list of other details all go into designing a piece of functional art. The concept must then be transformed into a stable and durable finished product that is both structurally sound and meets the client's size or functional specifications, all while recognizing the natural seasonal movement of wood. Designing just based on the wood, without a specific client and a specific budget in mind is fun, but this will not be your normal project scenario.

**"I could do it for that price" is also not your friend.** You may step into the studio of an urban craftsman or see their work at a show or gallery and think you could do the work for that cost. Possibly you could, but have you really considered the full cost? Thinking you could and doing are more distant relatives. Have you, for example, considered just the cost of the booth or gallery space and the time committed to showing you the product that craftsman is displaying, all in the hope of selling that item or another yet to be built?

Anyone in almost any trade can tell you that your actual time is higher than you think and your actual cost is higher than you anticipate; often using equipment you do not yet own in space you do not yet lease, all with utility bills and other overhead costs you cannot yet define.

Remember, as you start adding these various numbers up, only a small portion of your actual time will remain available for doing the actual woodwork. I run a shop with several full-time employees, so I enjoy far greater efficiency than a one or two-person business. Yet even at my scale, only 75 percent of my employee time is directly making progress on a client's project and, at most, a third of my personal hours are in contact with the wood. The balance of our time is spent on things that I would consider overhead tasks ranging from client meetings to cleaning, picking up log and supplies, shuffling wood from pile A to pile B just to get a look at the bottom board, maintaining tools and equipment shuffles. As a professional your hourly rates need to consider all these time and dollar costs.

As I was starting my business I met a woodworker at his

auction as he was closing his doors. He shared that he had made some mistakes in his early years working out of a garage. That was the mid-1980s and he thought $12/hour was pretty good money until he looked back and realized that wasn't even close to what operating his business actually cost. I felt pretty confident hearing this, because I was thinking my rate would be closer to $30/hour. I can now report (in hindsight) that my actual production rate in those early years was closer to $43/hour. I realize there are a dozen different ways to calculate what is overhead time or cost and what is direct project time or cost, but my point holds. If you think that a shop rate of $50 per hour in today's dollars will equate to a good checking balance at the end of the year, you may need to resharpen your pencil and think again.

**Faith, passion and perseverance are your friends.** Almost anything you read on the topic of business start-ups will tell you that it is not easy, and these same resources will tell you that most businesses fail. And yet people do it every day. Why, and especially why in a field that we have already laid out as one where you will not be getting rich? This is where passion comes into play. Most woodworkers understand this. Woodworking is a balance between creativity and skill, expressed on personal level and in a manner that can endure the test of time. It is why woodworking is a common hobby.

To move from hobby to business adds financial and time impacts that are not a fit for all. This is where faith comes into play. Faith of course has a broad range of meanings and implications, but from my perspective, all these broad meanings will be tested. I have a personal faith in a creator God and that is just one aspect of the faith to which I speak, and yes it was one factor in my quitting the day job to form my business. I recognize this might not be the case for all considering such a change, but being certain about what you believe and why goes a long way when times are trying.

Faith also needs to cover your confidence in your

technical skills as a sawyer, as a craftsman or in whatever aspect of this marketplace you feel led. This is likely the strength of anyone considering a woodworking business start-up, but your skills will likely forever be challenged if you do custom work. I've consistently found I need to be ready to bid jobs that I have never done before. I don't do so blindly, but I do need to develop a plan, define the process and determine the costs, all with enough confidence to convey that confidence to the client. And be certain this is not just about confidence, it is also about the ability to follow that confidence with action.

Finally, you need to have faith in your skills as a business owner/operator. Notwithstanding your best efforts, you will find there are many skills you had no idea you would even need. I, for example, was very confident in my technical skills and my ability to develop a solution without difficulties, but those are more the skills of an engineering introvert. I had very limited skills in the marketing arena. As a new business you certainly can start with the friends and family sales, but you will need to build a reputation and client base well beyond that to succeed.

And perseverance is the final detail in this set. There will be times when you could and should question whether this business is where you belong. For some, the question directly relates back to the various faith questions we just covered. For others it will simply be a money question in those times when the purse strings are tight. In the years since I started my business there have been many occasions where I faced plenty of uncertainty, the recession of 2008/09 being just one aspect. A strong network of honest advisors is one way in which passion and faith guide the perseverance test. Those that know you, your skills and your passions are also well equipped to advise in those more challenging times, as to whether your struggling business remains the best place for you, or not. Listen carefully, since the right answer may be the hard answer, whether that hard answer is to ride it out or pull the plug.

With all this in mind, a sequel to this book is in the planning stages. That sequel is aimed more at the "how to" of the urban wood business. I touched on this topic in Chapter 10 when I provided a case study of my business, The Wood Cycle. My business covers the full urban wood cycle from log to finished product. Not all urban wood businesses will or should follow this model. My plans for a sequel will be to cover all segments of the tree to table business in which I am engaged, in an attempt to guide future businesses in shaping a business model to their strengths and economic capabilities. To the extent that you think you may be part of this next chapter, send me a note and we will keep in touch.

**The Final Note**

Thanks for reading. I write this to an unknown audience, sharing my passion, but not knowing who might care. Such is each of our lives. And so it also goes for the urban trees beneath which we wander.

My observations over the years suggest that I have stumbled upon a topic upon which interest is gathering, and hence my effort to share these experiences and observations. I can only hope I have framed my thoughts constructively and in a manner that furthers the cause of our overall urban wood industry.

Whether this book sells five copies or multiple thousand is difficult to judge, so I welcome your responses back, but cannot promise whether I will be able to respond to just some or all. I do, after all, still have a business to run when I wake tomorrow morning, and who knows what tree may be calling.

# POSTSCRIPT

As I began writing this book, I realized the book was headed in two content directions; the "what of" and the "how to". What you now hold is the first of these; a background on how the urban wood industry came to be and how to connect with it. The second direction was more focused on the tricks of the trade and guidance on running an urban wood business. It was the things I have gleaned over the past 20 years of running my business. Chapters 7, 8, 14 and parts of several others contain hints of both as we tread the line between information that builds a more informed consumer and that which a maker of urban wood will be expected to know.

Once I realized these related but somewhat distinct audiences, I split the content based on the reader. I felt it more important to inform and grow our fan base before inviting more players on the stage. Seeing how this field has already grown over recent years, I have no doubt that second part will be needed soon.

If after this book you are considering such a direction, let us know and we will keep you tuned in to where we are headed. This second book will not provide all you need to know about running an urban woodworking business; but just as true, you can't run an urban woodworking business without much of the information that we have compiled through more than 20 years of experience. Some things you can only learn by experience, other things by reading. Through life most of us find a combination of the two seems the best approach.

*www.past9publishing.com*

# APPENDIX
## Urban Wood Candidate Log Criteria

**Desired Species (based on northern Midwest species):**

Apple (5' x 12" min.)
Ash
Birch
Butternut
Catalpa
Cherry
Elm (especially red/slippery)
Ginko
Hackberry
Hickory
Juniper (aromatic cedar)
Kentucky Coffee Bean
Locust-Black (12" min.)
Locust-Honey
Maple (Sugar, Black)
Mulberry (5'x12" min.)
Oak
Sycamore
Walnut
Burls of any species

Other historically significant trees and unusual ornamentals (size and quality depends on circumstances)

**Ideal Log Size/Quality:**

- 14" or larger small end diameter, measured inside the bark (smaller as noted for select species)
- 8' or longer (smaller as noted for select species)
- No limb scars for 7' (fresh cut or grown over)
- Straight or gradual curve in log
- No obvious rot or hollow (or minimal on very large diameters) (Note that a third and irregular darker color in the center of the log may be heart rot)
- Live or very recently dead when removed

**Conditionally Acceptable Log Size/Quality (based on supply & demand by species):**

- 12" to 14" small end diameter inside the bark with 2-3 minor limb scars
- 6' to 8' long if over 16" small end diameter if other logs also available on same trip
- 5' or longer if over 36" small end diameter, no rot
- 5' or long on walnut or cherry over 24"
- Limbs or other parts as discussed with arborist

**Species/Sizes Sometimes Accepted:**

- Silver and Norway Maples, Tulip Poplar, Basswood
- For these species, ideal logs only, 18" to 30" diameter, no rot

For approximate log diameter measurements, a man's fully extended hand-width (thumb tip to pinkie tip) is 8" to 9", so 1½ hand-widths measured across the end of a log is 14." For measuring a standing tree, a bear hug at chest height with hands overlapping for men or fingers touching for women) is about the equivalent log size.

# QUICK ORDER FORM

Online & Ebook Orders: www.past9publishing.com/shop/
Email Orders: past9publishing@gmail.com
Postal Orders: Past 9 Publishing
               1239 S Fish Hatchery Road
               Oregon, WI 53575

Name: _____

Address: _____

City: _____ State: _____ Zip: _____

Telephone: _____

Email Address: _____

**Number of copies** _____ x $19.95 = _____
*for orders of 10 or more copies check out our website for bulk pricing

**Shipping**  = _____
    $5.00 for the first book, $1.00 for each additional book
**Subtotal**  = _____

**Sales Tax**   subtotal x .055  = _____

**Total**  = _____

Make checks payable to Past 9 Publishing. We reserve the right to not ship books until your check has cleared your bank.

# QUICK ORDER FORM

Online & Ebook Orders: www.past9publishing.com/shop/
Email Orders: past9publishing@gmail.com
Postal Orders: Past 9 Publishing
               1239 S Fish Hatchery Road
               Oregon, WI 53575

Name: _____

Address: _____

City: _____ State: _____ Zip: _____

Telephone: _____

Email Address: _____

**Number of copies** _____ x $19.95 = _____
*for orders of 10 or more copies check out our website for bulk pricing

**Shipping**                                          = _____
       $5.00 for the first book, $1.00 for each additional book
**Subtotal**                                         = _____

**Sales Tax**    subtotal x .055             = _____

**Total**                                             = _____

Make checks payable to Past 9 Publishing. We reserve the right to not ship books until your check has cleared your bank.